FAST COMPANY

The
RULES
of Business

FAST COMPANY

The
RULES
of Business

55 Essential Ideas to Help
Smart People
(and Organizations)
Perform at Their Best

Fast Company's Editors and Writers

CURRENCY

DOUBLEDAY

NEW YORK   LONDON   TORONTO   SYDNEY   AUCKLAND

Contents

An Introduction to Where We Are Heading

"Play by the rules."
"There are no rules."

Well, which is it? On the one hand, if you've worked at a job anywhere for more than five minutes, you know that there are no hard-and-fast constructs to guarantee business success. What works brilliantly in one industry, in one organization, in one situation, may fail abysmally in the next. It's impossible to order and predict the vagaries of human nature or the chaos of the marketplace. The drama of business plays out in an ever-changing world—and in such a world, arguably, rules are what the unimaginative and the cowardly cling to as they're left behind.

And yet what if there *were* rules that, short of guaranteeing success, at least promised to point you in the right direction? What if you could tap the collected wisdom of the smartest business thinkers in history and distill a set of truths that applied most of the time, in most situations, to most people?

That's what this book is all about. The editors and writers of *Fast Company*, the magazine devoted to exploring how smart people work, have sought out the most important business ideas of all time. And from that encyclopedic trove, we've gleaned **The Rules.**

In the pages that follow, you will find more than 400 insights, imperatives, and hypotheses. You'll hear from plenty of luminaries, of course—from consultants and academics, but also from real-life executives leading companies that matter. There's Jeff Bezos of Amazon on the perils of hiring the wrong person; Intel's Andy Grove on seeing stars (and managing them); Bill Gates on the value of information technology; Anne Mulcahy of Xerox on managing change; Tom Peters on marketing Me, Inc.; and Michael Porter on (what else?) strategy. For the history buffs, we present Adam Smith and his invisible hand and Niccolò Machiavelli on the importance of reality checks.

But you'll also meet many surprising thinkers who come at business from unconventional perspectives. These are the unsung heroes and visionaries, people we've learned from who don't yet have high profiles but should. Read Vince McMahon, chairman of World Wrestling Entertainment, describe the worst sound in business. Doug Blevins, a wheelchair-bound pro football kicking instructor, speaks on the fallacy of trying to change people. There's luxury automobile dealer Carl Sewell on the profit imperative (straight talk from a car salesman!), and zookeeper Douglas Myers on communication and trust.

We have divided these excerpts into 22 sections that represent the most important business disciplines—from strategy to execution; from knowledge to speed. Each section is introduced by a brief essay that highlights themes and questions to guide you through what will follow. At the end of the sections, you'll find our "fast takes"—concrete guidelines, strategies, and tactics to help you immediately apply what you've just read to your work and life.

And **The Rules** themselves—well, you'll know them when you see them. We've carefully positioned them throughout this book. The first is, in some ways, the most important: Adapt or die. But we expect you'll find the 54 that follow almost as essential to you and your organization.

How best to use **The Rules**—and, for that matter, this book? Try taking it a section at a time. Highlight the quotes that grab you, and consider them in the context of the rules that precede or follow. Treat the "fast takes" as practical exercises to tease out and test what you've absorbed. How do **The Rules** make sense in your world? How can you apply them to make your work and life easier, more productive, and more satisfying?

Then use it as many readers do Fast Company. Keep it on your bookshelf, and come back to it as your work demands. (Many devoted subscribers still have our first issue—whose cover, incidentally, proposed the four "new rules of business.") Return to an especially pertinent section or a highlighted quote. Share it with colleagues and friends; start a discussion. Reconsider the text in terms of what you've experienced since last reading it. We don't have to tell you that change is constant; the rules apply only if you make them continually relevant.

Which brings us back to where we began. Are there "rules" that absolutely guarantee business and career success? Of course not. Life is not formulaic, and neither is business—which is what makes it so endlessly challenging and fascinating for us. There is no guarantee. We're expecting, though, that this book will sure increase your chances.

—Editors and writers of *Fast Company*

CHAPTER 1
Change

The 32-year-old company founder was tired as he sat down for a quick drink. He had done six fund-raising presentations in a row in the conference room downstairs, and the venture capitalists—still smarting from the burst of the Internet bubble—had been skeptical each and every time.

That explained his crankiness, and it could have also been the reason why he suddenly attacked the presentation his CEO a 30-year industry veteran had made earlier in the day.

#1

The first rule of business is the same as the first rule of life: Adapt or die.

"Right there, on his first slide, he wrote, 'Things change.' How could he say anything that trite?"

To his credit, the young hotshot was right. "Things change" is about as basic as a business cliché gets. But to dismiss the point out of hand is to ignore two vital facts:

1. There is a reason that sayings become clichés: They're often true.
2. The greatest cause of death among established companies is their inability to adapt to changing circumstances.

Companies have to constantly adapt and change. There is always both a looming threat as well as a massive opportunity in front of them. To ignore either is inevitably fatal.

Not surprisingly, then, change is a huge leadership challenge. Altering the direction of an organization is immensely difficult, and the problem is compounded by the fact that the people you depend on to execute the change—your employees—may not understand the reason why they have to do things differently. As a result, just when you need them most, they are likely to fight you at every turn.

And even if you convince them to go along, you must figure out how to change your organization effectively and in real time. In other words, you need to prepare for the future without screwing up the present.

No wonder change is difficult and why so many managers are unwilling to take on the task until it is too late. The inevitable result? Icons ranging from AT&T to Zenith ("the quality goes in before the name goes on") have been acquired by other companies—or have ceased to exist altogether.

Still, even a cursory survey of the best companies of all

time reveals that those organizations that survive for the long haul are constantly evolving in a myriad of ways. Two examples will suffice: The nature of GE's corporate portfolio seems to change almost daily, and PepsiCo, which began life selling just colas, gets the majority of its sales and earnings today from its Frito-Lay snack division.

But, as the business headlines remind us daily, those companies seem the exception. The wisdom of the leaders and thinkers in this book shows just how difficult change can be. It also reveals the upside: An organization that embraces change and executes it efficiently can evolve and thrive.

How change doesn't happen

"Picture an egg. Day after day, it sits there. No one pays attention to it. No one notices it. Certainly no one takes a picture of it or puts it on the cover of a celebrity-focused business magazine. Then one day, the shell cracks and out jumps a chicken.

"All of a sudden, the major magazines and newspapers jump on the story: 'Stunning Turnaround at Egg!' and 'The Chick Who Led the Breakthrough at Egg!' From the outside, the story always reads like an overnight sensation— as if the egg had suddenly and radically altered itself into a chicken.

"It's a silly analogy—but then our conventional way of looking at change is no less silly. Everyone looks for the 'miracle moment' when 'change happens.' But ask the good-to-great executives when change happened. They cannot pinpoint a single key event that exemplified their successful transition."

—Jim Collins, author, *Good to Great*

Speak to people's feelings

"How do you get people to change? The central issue is never strategy, structure, culture or systems. All those elements, and others, are important. But the core of the matter is always about changing the behavior of people, and behavior changes happen . . . mostly by speaking to people's feelings."

—John P. Kotter, former professor, Harvard Business School, and author of *Leading Change*

Change happens brick by brick

"Here's the problem with gradual: It's chronic, insidious and subtle. Half of all Americans are overweight? I can tell you how we got that way: one french fry at a time. We didn't foul the Love Canal in a week. That took a generation of dumping chemicals. Your company didn't hire 30 or 100 or 1,000 noncontributing employees all at once. That took years.

"The problem with gradual is that we don't notice the damage until the damage is extreme. And what happens when we finally do notice? Panic sets in. We put all our efforts into finding the quick fix.

"But here's the point of gradual. You don't win an Olympic gold medal with a few weeks of intensive training. There's no such thing as an overnight opera sensation. Every great company, every great brand, and every great career has been built in exactly the same way: bit by bit, step by step. If every element of an organization gets a little bit better every day, then the organization will become unstoppable."

—Seth Godin, author of *Unleashing the Ideavirus*

The most effective way to manage change is to create it

"To survive and succeed, every organization will have to turn itself into a change agent. The most effective way to manage change is to create it."

—Peter Drucker, sage

Only pissed-off people change the world

"Nearly 100 percent of innovation . . . is inspired not by 'market analysis' but by people who are supremely pissed off at the way things are. I happen to believe that only pissed-off people change the world, either in small ways or large ways."

—Tom Peters, co-author, *In Search of Excellence*

#2

Innovation is difficult and often painful. But there is no alternative. (See Rule 1: Adapt or die.)

Embrace change

"The minute you get good at something, you get comfortable. And that leads to stagnation. People on my team have learned to embrace change."

—Tamar Elkeles, vice president of learning, Qualcomm

Allow events to change you

"The prerequisites for growth are the openness to experience events and the willingness to be changed by them."

—Bruce Mau, founder, Bruce Mau Design

The more success you achieve

"The more success you achieve—either as an individual or as an organization—the more difficult it is to change. All of the learning that led to one kind of success becomes implicitly coded and works against your ability to unlearn. The challenge then becomes how to uncover those deeply ingrained assumptions."

—John Seely Brown, former director,
Xerox's Palo Alto Research Center (PARC)

#3

**When should you initiate change?
When things are going perfectly.**

The metabolism of change

"Change is not a process for the impatient. It takes time—a simple truth that many of us fail to realize. First, understand that the metabolism rate—the tolerance for change—in your boss or in your organization might be dramatically different from your own. Undoubtedly, others in your company feel as you do. Your task is to find them."

—Barbara Reinhold, director of career and
executive development, Smith College

If you don't like change

"If you don't like change, you're going to like irrelevance even less."

—General Eric Shinseki, former U.S. Army Chief of Staff

Change doesn't happen if you don't work at it.

"Change doesn't happen if you don't work at it. You've got to get out there, give people the straight scoop, and get buy-in. It's not just good-looking presentations; it's doing town meetings and letting people ask the tough questions. It's almost got to be done one person at a time."

—Anne M. Mulcahy, Chairman and CEO, Xerox Corp.

The faces that shape change

"Leaders ... must do more than just formulate strategies to exploit change. They must be able to help people understand the systematic forces that shape change."

—Peter Senge, author, The Fifth Discipline

The search for facts

"The big work behind business judgment is in finding and acknowledging the facts and circumstances concerning technology, the market and the like in their continuing changing forms. The rapidity of modern technological change makes the search for facts a permanently necessary feature of the industry. This seems obvious, but some of the biggest changes [for the worse] came about in part because someone got an idea that he thought was eternal."

—Alfred Sloan, the man who created General Motors

It makes sense to resist things that are a waste of time

"[Employees] know that . . . change itself is rarely for the better. If you've been with a company for a few years, and you've seen these flavor-of-the-month change programs come and go, you quickly recognize a pattern: Management launches some kind of change effort to great fanfare. Managers talk up the benefits and explain why this program will be good for both the company and its employees. They make promises, but at the end of the day . . . nothing really happens. . . . It makes sense to resist things that are a pure waste of time."

—Mark Maletz, author, *Creating the New Corporate Culture:*
A Handbook of Transformational Change

Why don't companies change?

"Why don't companies change? Let me give you an analogy from my own life. I am a fat smoker. I don't need another speech to tell me that I should stop smoking and lose weight.

"People in [companies] have heard all the speeches before too. Give great customer service, be a team player, manage your people. It's not that they don't believe the strategy. The problem is whether it's me giving up smoking or them starting to give great customer service, any kind of improvement requires short-term sacrifice and short-term pain in the name of a better long-term future. And there are very few businesses that are truly interested in maximizing their future income stream."

—David Maister, service industry guru and
author of *Managing the Professional Services Firm*

#4

Regardless of how realistic you think
you are being, the change process will
take three times as long as you like.

Never stop looking out the window

"I've driven through my share of rainstorms, listening to
some radio announcer in a windowless room telling me
that it's a sunny day. During a change in economic climate,
the biggest mistake a leader can make is not to recognize it.
So never stop looking out the window.

"When I ran Ronald Reagan's economic-policy board, I
met prominent CEOs who failed to recognize a change in
climate was in the offing. They looked at their current numbers, saw their order book was full, and believed everything
was terrific. But no graph goes up forever. That was true
then; it's true today. Recognize when the weather is shift-
ing. Rain or shine—look out."

—Walter Wriston, former CEO,
Citicorp/Citibank

FAST TAKE 1
HOW TO CHANGE

Like characters in Russian novels, all change initiatives are miserable in different ways. However, the way you should go about trying to change an organization is always the same:

1. Build the team.
2. Get the vision right.
3. Communicate for buy-in.
4. Empower action.
5. Create short-term wins.
6. Don't give up in the face of setbacks.
7. Make the changes stick.

These steps, of course, make change sound easier than it inevitably will be. Here is what former Harvard Business School professor John P. Kotter offers by way of tactics to make the process less painful.

See. Identify a problem, or solution to a problem, and then help people visualize it in a way that inspires positive action.

Feel. A dramatic, vivid visualization helps reduce the negative emotions that can block change.

Encourage. Eventually, the change initiative starts to build momentum. Do everything in your power to keep it going.

FAST TAKE 11
PERSUADING

A key part of your job as a leader involves changing people's minds, something that is incredibly hard to do.

Harvard University professor Howard Gardner, an expert on how people learn and deal with change, offers five specific ideas to help you engage with your employees to make the change process go more smoothly.

Connect with your audience. "Resonance," says Gardner, "is a union of reliability and trustworthiness." You can't control whether employees will like you, but you can—and must—do everything in your power to be trustworthy.

Level them with logic. Connecting with your audience is good, but you need to successfully make your case as well. Lay out your argument step by step, being as clear as humanly possible.

Know what you are up against. "It is essential for any leader to be aware of resistances," says Gardner.

Offer the carrot—cautiously. Reward the people who help promote the changes you want. But obviously, you need to be aware of false loyalty. "Rewards rarely change minds permanently," says Gardner.

Communicate widely and often. Present your message in a variety of forms and forums. Says Gardner: "The more representations you use, the more likely one will click."

CHAPTER 2
Communication

All the editors at *Fast Company* have developed a one-question test to assess the likelihood of a management theory working.

It doesn't matter if the person talking to us is a consultant discussing ways to streamline production (and thereby improve both efficiency and margins) or a CEO explaining that she has the answer to how her organization can gain a competitive edge in strategy, marketing, finance, or innovation.

Hearing the answer, we can—with uncanny accuracy—predict whether the idea being proposed will hold water in real life.

The question: "What about your employees?"

Invariably, every new management approach to strategy and tactics minimizes or ignores the people who are going to have to implement it: the organization's employees. And just as invariably the new initiative fails.

There is a perfect correlation.

#5

> **Employees need to know—in painstaking detail—what you want to do and why. They need to hear it again and again. Don't forget: It's impossible for them to hear it too often.**

The converse is also true: The more the person with the new idea has considered the role employees will play, the better the chances of success.

As you will see from the insights and reflections in this chapter, the best leaders are clear about three things:

1. For *any* program, project, or initiative to have a chance of succeeding, employees need to understand it completely. Making sure they do is a vital part of a manager's (or CEO's) job.
2. Despite what many (mediocre) managers and leaders believe, it is simply not possible to communicate too much.
3. Leaders must repeat over and over (and over) to employees where the organization is headed, how it is going to get there, and what the employees' roles are in helping make that happen.

It's all in the translation

"Communication is most effective when it translates a complex idea in a simple way."

—Mark Jarvis, senior vice president, Oracle

How to know what is really going on

"If you want to know what's really going on in most companies, you talk to the guy who sweeps the floors. Nine times out of 10, he knows more than the president. So, I make a point of knowing what my floor sweeps know— even if it means me sweeping the floors."

—Kenneth A. Hendricks,
CEO, ABC Supply Co.

Chief communications officer

"Leadership is an unbelievably hard communications job. You must have a firm grasp on your competitive environment, encapsulate the spirit of an organization, package it in strategic statements and then emphasize those statements repeatedly, so that the message becomes part of the conversation."

—Paul Danos, dean, Tuck School of Business,
Dartmouth College

Listen

"Begin a difficult conversation by listening. Don't just 'get right down to business.' Start with a few open-ended questions: 'How are you feeling?' 'How's it going?' And when the other person is talking, be quiet. The trust that you can build just by letting people say what they feel is incredible."

—Robert Buckman, chairman and CEO,
Buckman Laboratories, and author,
Building a Knowledge-Driven Organization

Face time

"An in-person visit beats a written memo every time."

—Byrd Baggett, entrepreneur and author,
Taking Charge

#6

If you can't communicate, you can't lead.

Leading well

"Every leader needs to clearly explain the top three things the organization is working on. If you can't, you are not leading well."

—Jeffrey Immelt, chairman and CEO,
General Electric

If you can't listen . . .

"If you can't listen, you don't have empathy—the ability to engage—and that's an incredible talent in business."

—Peter Crist, chairman, Crist Associates,
executive recruiters

They will only speak truth to power if . . .

"Upward communication only takes place when leaders are trusting and trustworthy."

—Douglas G. Myers, executive director,
San Diego Zoo

Clarity, conviction, and compassion

"For leaders, there is no trivial comment. The emotional wake that you leave behind is larger than you know. Speak with clarity, conviction and compassion. And above all, keep the conversation going."

—Susan Scott, author, *Fierce Conversations: Achieving Success at Work and in Life, One Conversation at a Time*

A leader's principal role is communication

"Strategy is really simple. The discipline to execute that strategy just requires discipline. A leader's principal role is communication."

Jonathan Schwartz, chief operating officer, Sun Microsystems

Relevance

"When presenting to senior execs, always focus on the past 90 days and the upcoming 90 days. Anything beyond that is irrelevant."

—Bill Jensen, consultant and author of *Work 2.0: Building the Future, One Employee at a Time*

It's impossible to overcommunicate

"It's virtually impossible to communicate too much. I've never heard any employee anywhere complain that he or she was being kept too informed."

—Jim Broadhead, former chairman and CEO, Florida Power and Light

You are the message

"When you communicate with someone, it's not just the words you choose to send to the other person that make up the message. You are also sending signals about what kind of person you are by your eyes, your facial expression, your body movement, your vocal pitch, tone, volume and intensity, and your sense of humor."

—Roger Ailes, president, Fox News

Why repetition works

"The first time you say something, it's heard. The second time, it's recognized, and the third time, it's learned."

—William H. Rastetter, chairman, Biogen IDEC

Understanding the story

"Whether you're talking about Wall Street, partners, customers, or employees, people must understand the organization's story—where it's headed, why you are making these changes, how you work, and how you think. Otherwise, you're going to lose valuation, sales, new opportunities, or employees."

—Gary Grates, executive director of
internal communications, General Motors

Words must be linked to deeds

"The wrong question is 'What do you want to say?' A better question: 'What do you want to accomplish?'"

—Michael Sheehan, president, Sheehan Associates,
communication consultants

#7

If you can't get your message across quickly, you aren't going to get it across at all.

Providing answers

"The most dangerous question a prospect or customer asks is 'Why should I?' And he may ask it more than once—but never of you. The product and its communication stream must continue to provide him with both rational and emotional answers."

—Lester Wunderman, father of direct mail advertising, founder of Wunderman Direct

PowerPoint isn't writing

"I love folks who can write well, because we in business have fallen too much in love with PowerPoint. PowerPoint isn't writing. It's a great tool, but it can become a great means of letting everybody stay in the river called Denial. It is a one-way communication. And writing a great paragraph requires that you state your point, that you back up your point, and you have a conclusion."

—Steve Murphy, CEO, Rodale

FAST TAKE
HOW TO COMMUNICATE

Michael Sheehan, a communications consultant, gets $15,000 a day to teach people how to get their message across. Here are eight things he says leaders absolutely must keep in mind.

Know your objective. Know your audience. This is the most important point of all. Before you start to craft your message, you need to know what you are trying to achieve. What effect do you want to have on your audience?

Three points . . . that is all anyone is going to remember. (Four at best.) What is the takeaway you want to leave them with?

Be animated. Odds are you're a lot duller than you think. "The key to the voice is overexaggeration," Sheehan says. "If you don't feel a little goofy, you're not doing it enough."

Make the first impression count. It colors everything that follows.

No rote. Yes, you have a message you want to get across, but you don't want to look and sound like a robot giving it. You want to come across as spontaneous and engaged, even if it's the twentieth time you have said the same thing.

Think in terms of sound bites. Memorable phrases help break through the clutter.

Trigger the "ooh." You need to figure out how you can get them to say, "Ooh, that's interesting."

Tell the truth.

CHAPTER 3

Creativity <u>and</u> Innovation

There is a reason we underlined the word *and* in the title of this chapter. The concepts of creativity and innovation need to be linked, harnessed together in a way that no one can separate them.

Invariably, when someone is trying to start a company or improve an existing one, they focus on either creativity or innovation, and the result, to be kind, is less than optimal.

#8

Nothing is more overrated than a new idea. Ideas by themselves are worthless. It's what you do with them that matters.

Clearly, to create something that has never existed before, you need the ability to look at one thing and see another. This is what we mean when we say, "I have a new idea."

But ideas themselves are worthless. You could come up with a dozen new ideas before breakfast if you gave yourself half a chance. ("Wouldn't it be great if we created a product that did X?" "You know, if we combined the features of Y and Z, we'd have a terrific service.") This might make for an entertaining game to play at your next company picnic, but it does not do anything to advance your business. The *concept* of cell phones had been around forever—they were featured in the Buck Rogers serials back in the 1930s—but cell phones didn't come into commercial use until half a century later. Until then, it was merely an intriguing idea. If you don't develop the idea, it remains just that, an idea.

The point is that you need to take ideas and do something with them. That is where the concept of innovation—developing ideas into useful products or services—comes in.

Can there be innovation without a new idea? Sure. Making a product "new and improved" qualifies as innovation. So does streamlining a production process. But incremental change rarely results in a huge competitive advantage.

True innovation occurs only when companies come up with a concept that has never existed before (the idea) and work to develop it into a commercial product or service—creativity *and* innovation.

The best leaders argue that creativity and innovation can be forced—that you can deliberately set out to create new products and services targeted for specific markets. That you can set budgets for innovations and expect results.

You may not be able to predict what will evolve, but it is fair to say, as leaders of some of the world's best companies do, "Five years from now I want one-third of sales to come from products that don't exist today"—and expect people to deliver on that vision.

An idea is just an idea

"An idea doesn't become an innovation until it is widely adopted and incorporated into people's daily lives."

—Art Fry, former corporate scientist, 3M,
and inventor of the Post-it note

Courage is the journey

"Before you can be creative, you must be courageous. Creativity is the destination, but courage is the journey."

—Joey Reiman, CEO, Brighthouse

What artists do

"My skill is the ability to put ideas together. If you give me a blank piece of paper, I will give you a blank piece of paper back. I find imitating and innovating a creative exercise. What I am able to do is take a couple of different ideas and merge them so they appear to be something different. And I think that is what artists do."

—Leslie H. Wexner, chairman and CEO,
Limited Brands

No straight lines

"No straight lines; no linear thinking."

> —Matthew Kissner, former president of
> Global Enterprise Solutions, Pitney Bowes

Innovation is not an event

"Innovation is not an event, a tool, or an application. It is an overall environment."

> Monte Ford, CIO, American Airlines

Innovation is a management function

"Innovation, like many business functions, is a management process that requires specific tools, rules and discipline—it is not mysterious."

> Tony Davila, Marc Epstein, and Robert Shelton

The breakthrough zone

"What not to do if you are trying to innovate: Fill a room with people from a single discipline. Or get a bunch of people from many disciplines and throw them all together. Either everyone has the same background, so it's hard to come up with big, surprising ideas, or people are so different they can't understand one another.

"Something magical happens when you bring together a group of people from different disciplines with a common purpose. It's a middle zone, the breakthrough zone."

> —Mark Stefik, research fellow and manager,
> Information Sciences and Technologies Laboratory,
> Palo Alto Research Center (PARC)

Don't underestimate the value of luck

"Don't underestimate the value of luck. I used to go to one of the first gourmet coffee bars in Portland. You could pull right up to the drive-through, and they would hand you coffee in a paper cup with a napkin wrapped around it. This was 1991.

"One morning I spilled the coffee in my lap. I didn't get badly burned, but I thought, 'Maybe there's a better way of doing this.'

"I don't think of myself as an inventor. But at the time, I was in real estate and on the verge of going broke. So I started playing around with paper [and eventually] sat down at my kitchen table and started wrapping insulated sleeves made from waffle-textured chipboard around paper cups."

—Jay Sorensen, founder, Java Jacket

In the age of the idea

"We're in the age of the idea. The organization that can develop a culture of creativity and idea generation will be the winner."

—Kevin Roberts, CEO, Saatchi & Saatchi

#9

If your cool new product or service doesn't generate enough money to cover costs and make a profit, it isn't innovation, it's art. If you covet awards, go to Hollywood.

Encourage innovation and edit

"Encourage invention and ideas, and then edit. It's about proliferation and promiscuity on the one hand—and then later, rigorous, tough-minded editing."

—Bruce Mau, founder, Bruce Mau Design

The keys to innovation

"There are two keys to innovation. The first is to think beyond relatively conventional paradigms and to examine traditional constraints using nontraditional thinking. You have to be able to go outside your own frame of reference and find another way to look at a problem. . . .

"The second key to innovation is the ability to discern the important issues and to keep your real goal in view. I don't think that we understood our real goal when we first started Federal Express. We thought that we were selling the transportation of goods; in fact, we were selling peace of mind. When we finally figured that out, we pursued our goal with a vengeance."

—Frederick W. Smith, chairman, president, and CEO, FedEx Corp.

Innovation is relative

"It's important to recognize that innovation is relative. It happens in companies of different sizes, at different levels. Innovation can be a clerk who finds a way to make filing 20% more efficient. It's important that we notice innovation, nurture it, and reward it."

—Simon Jeffery, former president and COO, LucasArts

Conventional wisdom

"Conventional wisdom says to get back to basics. Conventional wisdom says to cut costs. Conventional wisdom is doomed. The winners are the innovators who are making bold thinking an everyday part of doing business. It is the only way to win.

"You just can't grow revenue significantly unless you bring jaw-dropping new products and services to customers."

—Gary Hamel, chairman, Strategos, and co-author,
Competing for the Future

Equilibrium equals death

"Equilibrium equals death. Companies . . . may enjoy a period of time when equilibrium really works. It may give them a dominant position, and it may result in outstanding economic rewards. But it makes them increasingly vulnerable to the moment when the game changes. Because when the game changes, their winning formula from the previous period becomes their own worst enemy."

—Richard Pascale, co-author, Surfing the Edge of Chaos

A new environment

"Nothing sparks new ideas like a new environment."

—Ivy Ross, former head of design and
packaging for the girls' division, Mattel

Show me the results

"How do you demonstrate the value of innovation? By translating ideas into something that even skeptics can understand: results."

—Durwin Sharp, Virtual Thinking Expedition Co.

Brainstorming at ski lodges

"Brainstorming at ski lodges and beach resorts can be counterproductive. Do you want your team members to think that creativity and inspiration can only happen at high altitudes or within walking distance of an ocean? Don't get me wrong: Off-sites are fine. But remember, you want the buzz of creativity to blow through your offices as regularly as a breeze at the beach."

—Tom Kelley, president, IDEO

Customers can't tell you what they will need

"We cannot expect our customers to lead us toward innovations that they do not now need. Therefore, while keeping close to our customers is an important management paradigm for handling sustaining innovations, it may provide misleading data for handling disruptive ones."

—Clayton Christensen, author,
The Innovator's Dilemma

Being creative

"Once in a while, you lie awake thinking about all of the rules that you've learned—and feeling bad about having violated them. But if you're a truly creative person, you know that feeling insecure and lonely is par for the course. You can't have it both ways: You can't be creative, and conform too. You have to recognize that what makes you different also makes you creative."

—Arno Penzias, winner of the 1978 Nobel Prize
in physics and former chief scientist, Bell Labs

Stuck?

"The first step is admitting that you're stuck. If you can diagnose what's going on, you move to unstuck."

—Keith Yamashita, Stone Yamashita Partners,
co-author of Unstuck

#10

Make innovation pay its way. Business units should have to fund the research they want, instead of receiving a handout from corporate. Having to pay for it is a sure way to guarantee that the research is going to be focused.

Pay attention to ideas

"If you show that you truly pay attention to ideas—even the small, seemingly insignificant ones—then you'll create an environment in which people feel comfortable generating and offering them."

—Rolf Smith, Virtual Thinking Expedition Co.

Cubicle creativity

"If you want people to be creative, you have to put people in an environment that lets their imagination soar. Most people experience 'cubicle creativity': The size of their ideas is directly proportional to the space they have in which to think."

—Gerald Haman, founder, SolutionPeople

The prerequisites for innovation

"If you want to innovate, you need three things: a certain level of knowledge about your field; a great desire to do something useful; and an objective. Your objective may be broad or narrow, but you must have one. You must be willing to try different approaches to a problem, and you must not give up until you find an answer."

—Stephanie Kwolek, chemist,
inventor of Kevlar

Genius is . . .

"Genius is one percent inspiration, ninety-nine percent perspiration. Yes, sir, it's mostly hard work."

—Thomas A. Edison

Getting used to newness

"Humans need time to get used to newness, even if they themselves have created it. [For example], if you don't give designers time to get comfortable with their own creation, they will keep second-guessing the curve of a roof [of a car] or the shape of the grille even after it has been cast in metal."

—Chris Bangle, design chief, BMW

Outside the box?

"Being able to 'think out of the box' presupposes you were able to think in it."

—Robert A. Lutz, vice chairman, General Motors

Be clear

"Leaders need to be very clear about what kind of innovation they are looking for. One man's radical innovation is another man's incremental innovation."

—Alistair Corbett, director, Bain & Co., consultants

Creativity requires discipline

"The forgotten aspect of creativity is discipline. Anybody can be amusing and interesting and have clever ideas. What's hard is getting clever and interesting ideas into a product that's satisfying to consumers and is what the market is looking for and meeting your production deadline to get that product to the store when it's supposed to be there."

—John Riccitiello, former president and COO,
Electronic Arts

A faster horse

"If I had asked my customers what they wanted, they'd have said a faster horse."

—Attributed to Henry Ford

FAST TAKE ▌
CREATIVITY BY THE NUMBERS

Not sure where your next big idea will come from?

Evan I. Schwartz, author of _Juice: The Creative Fuel That Drives World-Class Inventors_, argues that the search may be simpler than you think.

Schwartz contends that new products fall into one of four categories:

**Offer a better mousetrap.** You take an existing concept and improve it.

**Recognize a latent desire.** Folks did not know they needed a Walkman until Sony unveiled it.

**Create something the world has been clamoring for.** Consider the lightbulb, airplanes, and cell phones.

**Result from a lucky break.** That was the case with the microwave oven, laser, and Post-it notes.

Simply understanding how breakthroughs occur could speed the creative process.

FAST TAKE 11
THE "RULES" FOR INNOVATION

"Pound for pound, the most innovative company in America is W. L. Gore & Associates," *Fast Company* wrote in December 2004. How does the company, which provides innovative solutions for the electronics, medical, and fabric industries (think Gore-Tex), do it?

W. L. Gore suggests there are six overarching keys:

Small teams. By keeping the size of working groups small, everyone gets to know one another and can work together with a minimal amount of rules.

No rank. Employees at W. L. Gore, who are called "associates," have "sponsors," who serve as mentors, not bosses. Associates decide for themselves what commitments to take on. Committees evaluate an associate's contribution to determine what the employee should be paid.

Take the long view. Developing revolutionary products takes time. Everyone at the company allows for that.

No chain of command. Anyone can talk to anyone. Memos and e-mail are discouraged. Face-to-face communication is preferred.

Everyone can lead. Associates spend about 10 percent of their time pursuing new ideas. Anyone can launch a project and be a leader.

Celebrate failure. When a project doesn't work out and the team kills it, they celebrate with beer or champagne, just as they would if it had been a success. Celebrating failure encourages risk taking.

CHAPTER 4

Customer Service

It should be a given that excellent customer service can be a significant competitive advantage.

Managers or companies that don't intuitively grasp this concept are missing something that is as basic as it is profitable: If you treat customers well, they will do more business with you. And what can be more important than that? Your company gets increased sales with lower marketing costs. (It is always less expensive to sell more to an existing customer than to create a relationship with a new one.)

#11

In the proverbial 10 words or less, here is the key to customer service: Ask customers what they want, and give it to them.

Providing superior customer service is a simple, straightforward way to improve your business. Take advantage of it. The best companies already do.

Moments of truth

"Last year, each of our 10 million customers came in contact with approximately five SAS employees, and this contact lasted an average of 15 seconds each time. Those 50 million 'moments of truth' are the moments that ultimately will determine whether SAS will succeed or fail as a company."

—Jan Carlzon, CEO, Scandinavian Airlines

Customer service *is* your job

"Customer relations is an integral part of your job—not an extension of it."

—William B. Martin, author, Quality Customer Service:
How to Win with the Customer

Don't hesitate

"If you want to keep their business, give customers exactly what they ask for—or even more—without any hesitation. If you do anything less, you might as well offer them nothing, because you'll have lost their good will."

—Carl Sewell, the world's most successful luxury
automobile dealer, and co-author, Customers for Life

Consistency

"You have to be consistent with all your customers. Inconsistent businesses have inconsistent profits."

—Jack Mitchell, clothier and author, Hug Your Customers

Selling is not about peddling a product

"Anyone who views a sale as a transaction is going to be toast down the line. Selling is not about peddling a product. It's about wrapping that product in a service—and about selling both the product and the service as an experience. This approach to selling helps create a vital element of the process: a relationship."

—Marilyn Carlson Nelson, co-chair, president, and CEO, Carlson Companies

Customer retention

"Customer retention requires customer satisfaction, but customer satisfaction is a moving target. Consumers as a whole are more demanding than ever, and rightly so. That means you must raise the service bar every time."

—The Disney Institute

You can't give good service if . . .

"Most people in business are committed to the customer in spirit, but lack the tools and tactics to fully embrace the commitment."

—Ben McConnell, co-author,
Creating Customer Evangelists

The source of competitive advantage

"Great customer service experiences are a source of long-term competitive advantage."

—Colin Shaw, co-author,
Building Great Customer Experiences

The most important person in the world?

"When you are speaking with a customer, who's the most important person in the world?

"'The customer,' you all say.

"Oh really? Let's look at it in a different way. Suppose there were only two people left on earth—you and the customer. One of you had to die. Who do you want to see drop dead?

"'The customer!' you all say.

"So now we have established that you are the most important person in the world. The problem is that when you are speaking with a customer, they think that they are the most important person in the world. It is your job to treat them that way."

—Jeffery Gitomer, consultant and author,
The Little Red Book of Selling

The one secret to giving great service

"You have to go eyeball to eyeball with your customers and say, 'Do I have a deal for you!' And then stand behind your product or service. Don't worry about stockholders or employees. If you take care of your customers, everything else will fall into place."

—Lee Iacocca, former president of both
Ford Motor Co. and Chrysler Corp.

Do *you* know what customers want?

"The closer top management is to the customer, the more successful an organization is likely to be."

—Dan Cathy, president and COO,
Chick-fil-A

The real cost of cost reduction

"Companies that focus on cost cutting must confront a simple truth that they prefer to ignore or deny: There is no such thing as a free cost reduction program. Any balance sheet will tell you that if you take from one side of the equation, you affect the other side. . . . The unasked question in a cost reduction program is who pays the price? Customers pay the price. Customers begin to see fewer unique and less differentiated products and fewer people to serve them. The people who stay on board to serve customers are not as excited or ambitious because morale is low.

"Cost reduction exacts an enormous price, and the prime target is . . . the consumer."

—Lior Arussy, author,
Passionate and Profitable

You can't give away the store

"As a service provider trying to solve customer problems, you need to be looking for the least expensive way to satisfy your customers. Sometimes serving a customer profitably is not possible, and we have to turn away the business."

—Jeff Gee and Val Gee, authors, *Super Service:
Seven Keys to Delivering Great Customer Service*

There is always something you can improve

"When you focus on your customers, you're never satisfied. There's always something you can improve."

—Debora Wilson, president, The Weather Channel

You are the company

"Customers don't distinguish between you and the organization you work for. Nor should they. To your customer's way of thinking, you are the company. Customers don't know how things get done behind doors marked 'employees only.' They don't know your areas of responsibility, your job description, or what you can and cannot personally do for them. And they don't care. To customers, those things are your business, not theirs."

—Ron Zemke, co-author,
Delivering Knock Your Socks Off Service

Where business is won and lost

"Customer experience is the next competitive battleground. It's where business is going to be won or lost."

—Tom Knighton, executive vice president,
Forum Corp., consultants

FAST TAKE

WORK TO GET A GREATER SHARE OF YOUR CUSTOMER'S WALLET

The natural inclination is always to increase your marketing budget in order to attract new clients.

That makes perfect sense, of course. The more money you spend on marketing, the more customers you tend to attract. The more customers you attract, the higher your revenues.

But as logical as going after new customers may be, it could be an expensive mistake.

Odds are there is plenty more business you could be doing with your existing customers—additional business you can obtain for far less than going after new markets.

The moral: Before you rush out to find additional clients, first try to turn one-time buyers into lifetime customers.

Why?

Well, if you do, five things happen, all of them good:

It is easier to sell to an existing customer than to a new one. As we stated earlier, you already have forged a relationship with them; they're your customer, after all. In addition, you don't have to spend money to figure out whom you want to sell to. You already know. The net result: Your marketing costs go down.

You don't have to spend as much on marketing to reach them; you already have a relationship. They will pay more attention to your marketing messages, since they already know you.

If the customer is buying from you, they are not buying from the competition. By turning one-time buyers into lifetime customers, you are helped, while your competition is hurt.

Repeat customers are (slightly) less price sensitive. They are willing to pay a (small) premium for doing business with you, because you have forged a positive relationship. It is worth it to them to pay a bit more to keep from searching for another vendor who may or may not serve their needs as well.

They will be more willing to try a second, different product you have to offer than to sample a product from someone with whom they have no relationship. The trust you have built up by selling your customer the first product or service will spill over to offering number two.

Selling more to your existing clients is a far better and cheaper marketing strategy than finding new ones.

If you are not trying to get the biggest share of your customer's wallet, you are costing yourself money. Probably a lot of money.

Here's a simple example. Let's say you sell cars for a living. To keep the math simple, let's say the average price of a car rolling off your lot is $25,000.

Over the course of a lifetime, an average customer buys 10 new cars. So that comes to $250,000 in revenues (in current dollars).

Buyers tend to shell out about a third of the price of the car in maintenance over time—everything from oil changes to fixing fender benders. That is another $82,500 or so, to bring the grand total of spending directly related to purchasing a car to $332,500. That is how much converting one car buyer into a lifetime customer could generate in revenue for you over time.

Put another way, a person can spend $25,000 for a car and never darken your door again. Or they could do all their car buying from you during their lifetime, giving you a total of $332,500.

The difference is $307,500. How many radio and television spots and end-of-the-model-year sales do you have to hold to bring in an additional $307,500 in revenue?

It is hard to imagine any marketing campaign generating a return equal to what you can get by trying to convince your existing customers to buy more from you.

Before you start looking for more customers, make sure you are getting as much revenue out of your current customers as you can.

Call up the 10 customers who account for the largest percentage of your revenues, thank them for their business, and start a conversation about what else you can do to make their lives easier.

CHAPTER 5

Decision Making

You would be hard pressed to find someone who would disagree with the statement that employees at just about every level of the organization need to be able to make decisions. But teaching people that skill gets remarkably short shrift.

We offer the people who work for us training in everything else: sales, marketing, finance, how to deal with fellow employees (difficult or otherwise). Why not teach them the best way to make a decision?

It seems logical, but too many companies don't do it.

When we ask managers at struggling or underperforming organizations why their companies don't offer such training, the answer we usually hear is something along the lines of "If you've explained to people how to do their jobs, they'll know what to do when the time comes."

#12

"No" is the second best answer you can get to any question you ask.

But that is just silly. Since it is impossible to come up with a complete list of what might happen, you can't train people for every contingency.

So what are employees supposed to do when they are confronted with the unanticipated?

Though formal decision-making training is hard to come by, the best managers have given the matter serious thought. Some of their wisdom follows.

Decisions, by themselves, are meaningless

"People confuse making a decision with making something happen. And so we work at making good decisions. Did we have all of the information to make the decision? Is it possible that a better decision could have been made if better information had been produced?

"Well, it's always better to make a good decision than a bad decision, but just making a decision doesn't change anything! A decision is the beginning of the process of doing, not the end of that process. The question is: Did you implement the decision? Did you actually do anything?"

—Jeffrey Pfeffer, professor, Stanford Graduate
School of Business

#13

Not deciding is a decision. That's the problem with procrastinating.

Debating is easy

"Making and implementing decisions boils down to a key ingredient: listening. I often wonder why schools emphasize debating. Why not have listening classes as well? Debating is easy; listening with an open mind is not. The worst thing that you as a leader can do in the decision-making process is to voice your opinion before anyone else can. No matter how open and honest your people are, stating your opinion first will shortchange the discussion process and taint what you hear later."

—Deborah Triant, former president and CEO,
Check Point Software

Trust your gut

"You know more than you think you do."

—Dr. Benjamin Spock

Intelligent compromises

"The enemy of 'good' is 'perfect.' When time is critical, you have to make intelligent compromises."

—O. Wayne Isom, professor, Weill Medical College,
Cornell University

You must make money

"You always focus on profitable contribution. When you enter new markets, by definition, the initial profit contribution won't be what you'll want to see later, but you've got to keep your culture focused on profit growth. This is what got the dotcoms in trouble. It will get successful companies, including Cisco, in trouble too if people make the mistake of focusing on market-share gain and not on understanding profitability."

—John Chambers, CEO, Cisco Systems

Provide context

"If you look closely at how people make decisions, a clear pattern emerges. No matter what the new strategy, initiative, or change program is, people have the same questions: How is this change relevant to what I do? What, specifically, should I do? How will I be measured, and what consequences will I face? What tools and support are available? What's in it for me?

"The leader's job is to help people answer those questions. After all, if people can't answer those questions on their own, then the grapevine will provide the answers—and those answers won't always be right."

—Bill Jensen, consultant and author, *Simplicity: The New Competitive Advantage in a World of More, Better, Faster*

The way to bet

"The race does not always go to the swift, nor the battle to the strong—but that's the way to bet."

—Damon Runyon, author, *Guys and Dolls*

Use your intuition

"Use your intuition. I define intuition as the way we translate our experience into action. Our experience lets us recognize what is going on (making judgments) and how to react (making decisions). Because our experience enables us to recognize what to do, we don't deliberately have to think through issues to arrive at good decisions quickly."

—Gary Klein, consultant and author,
The Power of Intuition

When your intuition is out of sync with analysis

"Here's an interesting thought experiment: You've got to decide between two things—two executives to hire for a key position, two acquisition targets. You identify all of the factors, weighing each alternative, and your analysis says to pick A over B. But your intuition says to pick B over A. So what do you do?

"Most people will go on their intuition—which raises the question: Why did you do all that work in the first place? One of these two options is wrong. So postpone your decision until you can determine why your intuition is out of sync with the systematic analysis."

—Max Bazerman, professor,
Harvard Business School

How to make better decisions

"If people have better information, they make better decisions—period."

—Suzanne Muchin, CEO, Civitas

Learning from experience

"You need to learn from your experiences. We regularly meet to discuss grant proposals that we've turned down. It's an opportunity to ask . . . Are we missing something important here?"

—Richard Klausner, executive director,
Global Health Program,
Bill & Melinda Gates Foundation

The invisible hand

"Every individual endeavors as much as he can to employ his capital to produce . . . what will be of the greatest value [to him]. He . . . neither intends to promote the public interest nor knows how much he is promoting it. . . . He intends only his own security; and by directing that industry in such a manner as it may produce the greatest value, he intends only his own gain, and he is in this, as in many other cases, led by an invisible hand to promote an end which was no part of his intention. . . . By pursuing his own interest he frequently promotes that of society more effectively than when he really intends to promote it."

—Adam Smith, eighteenth-century economist

Intuition

"Intuition is part experience and part talent. Your intuition—your ability to know what's right—should become sharper over time."

—Freeman Thomas, director of strategic design,
Ford Motor Co.

Try not to make decisions for others

"As a leader, I try not to make decisions for others. Sure, being a dictator is often the fastest way to get things done. But it's not a process that allows an organization to sustain growth. I want the people in my organization to learn the lessons that come with making decisions: that everything is a compromise, that nothing is ever completely logical, but that you can deal with things through a logical decision-making process."

—Pamela Lopker, founder and president, QAD

#14

It is extremely hard to make a list of all the things you haven't thought of. That explains why it is important to open up the decision-making process to as many people as possible.

Just-in-time decisions

"If you are not going to do anything different tomorrow by making a decision today, then don't make it today. Situations change; markets shift. That's not an excuse to procrastinate. But the best decisions are just-in-time decisions. You should decide as late as possible."

—David House, executive chairman,
Brocade Communications Systems

Intuition will lead you astray

"When making a decision, don't listen to your intuition. Intuition will lead you astray; it's drastically overrated. The desire to follow intuition reflects the mythology of people who don't want to think rationally and systematically. Often, when you hear about intuition, what you're really hearing is a justification of luck. Intuition might be fine for the small decisions in life—like what kind of ice cream to buy. But when you get to the biggies, you need a more systematic thought process."

—Max Bazerman, professor,
Harvard Business School

Why meetings are ineffective

"Meetings are ineffective because they lack contextual structure. Too many organizations have only one kind of regular meeting, often called a staff meeting. Either once a week or twice a month, people get together for two or three hours of randomly focused discussion about everything from strategy to tactics, from administriva to culture. Because there is no clarity around what topics are appropriate, there is no clear context for the various discussions that take place. In the end, little is decided because the participants have a hard time figuring out whether they're supposed to be debating, voting, brainstorming, weighing in, or just listening."

—Patrick M. Lencioni, author of *Death by Meeting*

FAST TAKE
HOW TO MAKE A DECISION

Are you absolutely certain that you know the best way of making a decision? If not, J. Edward Russo of the Johnson Graduate School of Management at Cornell and Paul J. H. Schoemaker of the Wharton School at the University of Pennsylvania, authors of *Winning Decisions: Getting It Right the First Time*, can help.

They break down the decision-making process into four discrete steps:

1. *Framing,* that is, deciding what you are going to decide—and not decide.
2. *Gathering intelligence:* real intelligence, not just information that will support internal biases.
3. *Coming to conclusions,* which is another way of saying acting on the intelligence you gather.
4. *Learning from experience,* because the only thing worse than not knowing how to make a decision is having to make the same decision over and over again.

CHAPTER 6

Welcome to the Design Revolution

Design isn't a word that most people associate with business experiences, services, and customer satisfaction. Nor is it something that they automatically tie to innovation and competitive advantage. But they should.

#15

Design will be the next place companies battle for competitive advantage.

Design is a new way of thinking about the way we lead, manage, create, and forge relationships with the people we will sell to.

Yves Behar, who works with Nike and Toshiba, believes that design can be used to strike an all-important emotional connection with customers. Only by establishing such a connection, he argues, can you ensure their loyalty to your products.

In years gone by, the way companies forged that kind of relationship was through one-to-one selling. Given the expense, those days are almost completely gone. You used to create those relationships—to some extent—with advertising. But given the proliferation of both media (for example, cable, Internet, satellite radio, television, and the Internet) and the number of messages we are subjected to each day, that too is no longer as effective.

Today, one of the few ways you can show consumers directly what your company stands for is through the design of your product (think Apple). That design is reinforced by what your packaging, ads, and Web site look like.

In the pages that follow you'll see what some of today's foremost leaders and thinkers make of the relationship between design and business strategy.

Design isn't an abstraction

"Design isn't an abstraction—it's a direct manifestation of your philosophy and your attitude. That's why people want to see the Web page and look around the office when they are thinking about joining a company. They think, 'I fit here,' or they think, 'I don't fit here.' Design speaks volumes about a company's culture. It tells you if a company is egalitarian or if it's hierarchical, if it's easygoing or if it's uptight.

"How a company chooses to translate its values into design is enormously important."

—Rolf Fehlbaum, CEO, Vitra

Appealing to hearts and minds

"If you can design a product that appeals to people's brains and hearts, you can get them to pay a great premium."

—Alex Lee, president, OXO International

Good design is good business

"I became a believer in design early in my career. Back in 1984, we introduced Liquid Tide, and one of the most critical pieces of the new product was the cap. It measures and has a self-draining device so that it is not messy. I was part of the team that designed the cap. We thought it was a small thing. But women who used the product appreciated it. You don't appreciate Tide's cleaning ability in every laundry load. But you appreciate the design of the cap every time you use the laundry detergent.

"When I became chief executive, I had the opportunity to lead my personal crusade for design. In the past, our innovation process was sequential, and it usually started either with a consumer insight or, more likely, a technology invention. We'd confirm the concept, engineer the product and then get design and marketing involved.

"Where we consciously involved design at the front end we generated more trial, more repurchase and more sales. Why? We delivered delightful consumer experiences.

"Design can unlock the technological performance we build into a product and help the consumer see it, touch it. I am not doing this because I am a frustrated liberal arts major. Good design is good business."

—A. G. Lafley, chairman, president, and CEO,
Procter & Gamble

#16

Yes, it is important to be innovative,
eye-catching, and fun. But if consumers
can't easily use your design,
they won't buy your product.

Breaking through the clutter

"In a crowded marketplace, aesthetics is often the only way to make a product stand out. Quality and price may be absolutes, but tastes still vary and not every manufacturer has learned how to make products that appeal to the senses."

—Virginia Postrel, author, *The Substance of Style*

Form is function

"It's said that form follows function. I disagree. Form is function. The two are developed together and are intertwined. In a truly great design—a design that stands the test of time—that is done as efficiently as possible. A great design has nothing more than it needs to do the job."

—Davin Stowell, founder, Smart Design

98 percent common sense

"Good design is probably 98 percent common sense. Above all, an object must function well and efficiently—and getting that part right requires a good deal of time and attention."

—Sir Terence Conran, chairman, Conran & Partners

Developing great products

"It takes [the same amount of] resources to develop a mediocre product as a great one."

—Jonathan Cagan and Craig M. Vogel, authors,
Creating Breakthrough Products

Customers appreciate good design

"Customers appreciate good design. While they can't necessarily point out the attributes of what it is, they know it feels better, is better. There's a visceral connection. They are willing to pay for it, if you give them a great experience. You will find those better-designed examples—like the Apple iPod—achieving greater value."

—James P. Hackett, president and
CEO, Steelcase

Design for profit

"In the product-centric world of the past, profit was an outcome of strong market share. Companies focused on one goal: Sell more to anyone willing to buy. Companies generated revenue on each unit sold. How the company benefited from those sales was all but taken for granted. Today, product is not just generated by the products a company sells, and profit cannot be taken for granted. Today, product is an outcome of smart business design. In fact, the value recapture of business design—the 'how do I get paid' dimension—is one of the most critical components."

—Adrian Slywotzky, managing director,
Mercer Management Consulting

Sifting through sand for seashells

"Design is like sifting through sand for seashells. The human brain sifts images and bits of type. It innately simplifies and groups similar elements. If it cannot easily make these connections it perceives confusion."

—Alexander W. White, author,
The Elements of Graphic Design

Show the future

"Designers have a responsibility to show the future as they want it to be—or at least as it can be, and not just the way an industry wants it to be."

—Yves Behar, founder, fuseproject, a San Francisco–based
design and branding firm

How to design an office

"To maximize the amount of contact among employees, you really ought to put the most valuable staff members in the center of the room, where the highest number of people can be within their orbit. Or, even better, put all places where people tend to congregate—the public areas—in the center, so they can draw from as many disparate parts of the company as possible. Is it any wonder that creative firms often prefer loft-style buildings, which have usable centers?"

—Malcolm Gladwell, author, *The Tipping Point*

Attractive things work better

"Attractive things do work better. Their attractiveness produces positive emotions, causing mental processes to be more creative, more tolerant of minor difficulties."

—Donald A. Norman, author,
The Design of Everyday Things

Becoming a design leader

"Once primarily known for its low prices, Target has become a design leader. Teaming up with famed architect Michael Graves, Target introduced a whimsical housewares line. The wildly successful Graves Collection proved contagious and eventually included some two hundred items in various product categories such as garden furniture and timepieces. More than just introducing design for the masses, Target was determined to break out of its decades-old idea of a discount store."

—Tom Kelley, managing director, IDEO,
and author, *The Art of Innovation*

An enterprise's most vital assets

"An enterprise's most vital assets lie in its design and other creative capabilities."

—Kun-Hee Lee, chairman and CEO,
Samsung Electronics

The highest calling

"I define the highest calling of creative work as producing new forms or designs that are readily transferable and widely useful. . . . Not just building a better mousetrap, but noticing that a better mousetrap would be a handy thing to have."

—Richard Florida, professor, Carnegie Mellon University,
and author, *The Rise of the Creative Class*

A voice at the table

"Designers need to be a voice at the table from the beginning so they can identify where and why design can make a difference. They also need to understand the business issues, that if we don't make our numbers this quarter we don't earn the right to do something [cool] the next time."

—Chuck Jones, head of design, Whirlpool Corp.

ACCEPTING THE IMPORTANCE OF DESIGN

How do you get your organization to accept the importance of design, especially risky (i.e., break-through-the-clutter) design? Patrick le Quément, Renault's design chief, suggests:

Build on existing strengths. If you can point out that the design in question logically builds off what the organization has done in the past, it is an easier sell.

Don't keep repeating yourself. Respect for the past doesn't mean being stuck in it. "Anything retro is retrograde," says le Quément. "It's driving while looking in the rearview mirror, admitting you have run out of ideas."

Sell the idea every way you can think of. "We publish books, write reports and make films so that we have the intellectual presence to participate in the debate," le Quément says.

Broadcast your ideas. Let people inside the organization see what you are thinking about. Show them where you want to go.

FAST TAKE 11
LESSONS FROM THE DESIGN MASTERS

It is hard to find two companies that have the same approach to design. However, if you talk to enough of them, certain commonalities appear.

Design is the differentiator. Companies that believe in design know that it gives them a distinctive look and feel that separates them from the pack.

Make it real. While Target had the foresight to bring high-concept design to the masses, it still needed to translate inspiration into real products that real people would use.

Design defines who you are. All-star architect William McDonough started designing environmentally sustainable products. Those who adopted his ideas—companies such as Herman Miller and Berkshire Hathaway's Shaw Industries—are telling the world what they think is important.

CHAPTER 7
Execute!

A funny thing happened on the way to the New Economy, the place where only ideas would matter in business and everything else would become a commodity. It turns out that ideas alone aren't worth much. You need to turn them into a profitable reality.

In other words, whether you are in the new economy or old, you need to execute. Companies that don't soon disappear.

If you don't execute, you won't accomplish a thing.

Most senior managers don't execute well. Perhaps they don't want to get their hands dirty with the details.

But, as what you are about to read makes clear, often the difference between a company and its competitors is the ability to execute.

For all the talk about competing in "an idea economy" and "concentrating on what you do best and outsourcing the rest," companies still actually have to get the work done well.

You either do that or watch as your organization steadily falls behind those who do. The major difference between Dell and every other maker of personal computers isn't the technology—they all basically offer the same processors, memory, and the like. It is that Dell has figured out how to make it simple to buy a reliable computer for less money and everyone else has not.

Either you learn how to execute or you (eventually) fail.

Execution is . . .

"Execution is the ability to mesh strategy with reality, align people with goals, and achieve the promised results."

—Larry Bossidy, former CEO, Allied Signal and
Honeywell, and co-author, *Execution*

#18

Hold people accountable. Reward those who execute. Coach those who don't. And if they still don't get it, fire them. You aren't helping them, or the organization, by having them stick around.

Execution beats strategy every time

"A half-baked strategy well executed will be superior to that marvelous strategy that isn't executed very well."

—Allan Gilmour, vice chairman,
Ford Motor Co.

Focus

"As a senior manager, you have many choices about what to do. But one thing you must do: choose. Get your organization focused on, committed to, and acting on a few crucial big goals."

—Robert A. Neiman, author,
Execution Plain and Simple

Follow up on everything

"Unsuccessful commanders issue orders and then return to their card games at headquarters. They believe the simple act of issuing an order will immediately cause everything to fall into place, and the battle will go their way just because they said so. They expect everything to go exactly according to their plans. That is as unrealistic as it is stupid. A successful commander issues an order and then makes damn sure it's not only carried out but working as planned. If things go wrong, or a situation changes, the commander will be aware of it immediately and be able to change the orders in response. . . . Don't jump to conclusions and don't make assumptions. Follow up on everything."

—General George S. Patton

The next steps

"Connect every message with an action to be taken or a plan to be implemented. If your constituents are expected to make changes, they need to understand how to do that, and what the next steps are."

—Mike Freedman, author, The Art and
Discipline of Strategic Leadership

Doing good is good business

"You don't have to spend a jillion dollars on advertising to get your word out. What matters is that customers have a good experience with your product at every single point of contact. We completely obsess about execution. Doing good is good business."

—David Neeleman, founder, JetBlue

When excellent execution does not matter

"If the concept is not well thought through and does not properly identify the market then even excellent execution of the program will not matter."

—Jeffrey Liker, author, The Toyota Way: 14 Management Principles
from the World's Greatest Manufacturer

Never disappoint your customers

"Develop and maintain flawless operational execution. You might not always delight your customers, but make sure never to disappoint them."

—Nitin Nohria, professor, Harvard Business School; William Joyce,
professor, Tuck School of Business, Dartmouth College; and
Bruce Roberson, executive vice president, Safety-Kleen

Just do it

"When Nike chose 'Just Do It' as their advertising slogan, they hit upon a true component of the success formula—the importance of execution. No matter how hard and long you plan, when it comes to where 'the rubber meets the road,' as another advertising slogan said, the plan doesn't serve you until it's put into place.

"This is the major difference between the successful person and the also-ran (or never-ran, if there is such a phrase). The successful person puts his or her plans into effect, where the unsuccessful one may plan up a storm, but never does anything about it—or if they do start, they do it only halfway.

"Nothing gets better until someone actually does something."

—Daryl R. Gibson, salestar.com

Faster, cheaper, and better

"If you can consistently do your work faster, cheaper and better than the other guy, then you get to wipe the floor with him—without any accounting tricks."

—Michael Hammer, consultant and co-author,
Reengineering the Corporation

Optimism can't outweigh execution

"Optimism cannot outweigh execution. A lot of people who jumped into new opportunities in the 1990s not only lacked discipline, they lacked experience. They're gone now."

—Ann Winblad, co-founding partner,
Hummer Winblad, venture capitalists

Knowing isn't the same as doing

"Advocates of knowledge management as 'the next big thing' have advanced the proposition that what companies need is more intellectual capital. While that is undeniably true, it's only partly true. What those advocates are forgetting is that knowledge is only useful if you do something with it."

—Jeffrey Pfeffer, professor,
Stanford Graduate School of Business

Be ruthless

"Execution. For a proven business, it is about performing at or above known standards. Many large, established organizations are able to sustain success because they are ruthless about holding their managers accountable to meeting or exceeding standards."

—Vijay Govindarajan, Tuck School of Business,
Dartmouth College

EXECUTION FOR DUMMIES

Just because you tell someone to do something doesn't mean it's going to get done.

Larry Bossidy and Ram Charan hammered home the point that you need to see an idea through to the finish in their best-seller *Execution: The Discipline of Getting Things Done*. But how exactly you are supposed to do that has remained fuzzy.

Laurence Haughton, who wrote *It's Not What You Say ... It's What You Do*, has set out to provide a framework for making execution simpler, based on the experiences of several dozen successful companies.

To Haughton, there are four discrete elements required to execute efficiently:

1. *Be clear about what you want to accomplish.* Too often managers are vague and confusing because they don't take enough time to explain what needs to be done, or don't check to see that what they are saying is what the people under them are hearing. If things start to go off track, don't immediately assume the strategy was wrong. Double-check to see that everyone understood what was supposed to be done.

2. *Match people to the task at hand.* Will the job call for problem solving or going by the book? Will people be operating on their own or under constant supervision? Are there likely to be a lot of obstacles, or is the task relatively straightforward? Ask yourself these questions upfront, says Haughton, and staff the project accordingly. Haughton also argues that a person's attitude (i.e.,

whether they want to tackle the task at hand) is at least as important as their experience.

3. *Make sure they buy in.* Unless employees see the importance of the task, and want to accomplish it, there is little chance anything will be accomplished. To overcome resistance, Haughton argues for launching new initiatives with a lot of hoopla, following through immediately to sustain momentum, and singling out those doing the best job. (It sends the message that management is watching closely.)

4. *Keep them fired up.* Even the most enthusiastic team member can lose heart when things take longer than expected or when they encounter obstacles. To ensure that people stay engaged, make sure they "own" the new initiative. You do that by sharing information, pushing authority as far down the ranks as possible, and encouraging disagreement to make sure the best ideas surface.

CHAPTER 8

Hiring *and* Developing *and* Retaining Great Employees

W e'll be honest. We didn't expect to see it in our lifetime. We never thought that companies could come close to living up to what has become the ultimate business cliché: "Our employees are our most important asset."

Yes, CEOs and senior managers have been saying that for at least twenty-five years, and yes, smaller companies as well as many of those that *Fast Company* writes about on a regular basis have always taken the care and feeding of their employees seriously.

#19

No matter how overwhelmed you are
with work, it is *always* better to hire
no one than to hire the wrong person.
It sounds so basic, but the rule is
violated every day everywhere—with
disastrous results.

But in recent years the trend, thankfully, has become more pervasive. Just about every company is spending more time and money on recruiting, trying to find the absolutely best people. Potential hires are being subjected to more interviews and are being tested more extensively, according to nearly every company we talk to.

That's a good first step, but it is only one-third of the battle.

If employees really are your company's most important asset, doing nothing to further their abilities and careers once you have hired them is like buying a home and doing nothing to maintain or upgrade it. You are letting your asset go to waste.

And even if you make the commitment to hiring the best and nurturing their development, there is still one more giant step to take: You need to make sure that you hold on to your best people. If you truly believe they are the reason for your success, you need to make sure they stick around.

As the leaders you are about to hear from know, hiring the best people is good. Hiring good people and developing them to their fullest potential is better, and hiring and developing good people and making sure they stay with your company is best.

We can't think of a better message to impart.

Have your best do the hiring

"Most companies have people who have never served in the trenches do their hiring. They call it H.R. I call it crazy. Only the top 10 percent of the Corps gets a shot at recruitment duty. These people are the real thing. Recruiting is all about creating a clear picture of your organization. The best way to do that is to put the best product of that organization in front of potential recruits."

—Andy Brown, master sergeant, U.S. Marine Corps

No bozos

"The best thing we can do for our competitors is hire poorly. If I hire a bunch of bozos, it will hurt us, because it takes time to get rid of them. They start infiltrating the organization and then they themselves start hiring people of lower quality."

—David Pritchard, director of recruiting,
Microsoft

A pipeline of talent

"How can you build a pipeline of talent—the only thing that's going to help you over time—if you put out a search only when you have a position to fill?"

—Rusty Rueff, executive vice president for
human resources, Electronics Arts

Hire right

"I'd rather interview 50 people and not hire anyone than hire the wrong person. Cultures aren't so much planned as they evolve from that early set of people. New employees either dislike the culture and leave, or feel comfortable and stay, so the culture becomes self-reinforcing and very stable."

—Jeff Bezos, CEO, Amazon.com

You've got to give people a voice

"You've got to give people a voice in their jobs. You've got to give them a piece of the action and a chance to excel. You've got to give them a chance to have fun."

—Mike Cudahy, founder,
Marquette Electronics

How to be successful dealing with people

"When people walk in the door, they want to know: What do you expect out of me? What's in this deal for me? What do I have to do to get ahead? Where do I go in this organization to get justice if I'm not treated appropriately? They want to know how they're doing. They want some feedback. And they want to know that what they are doing is important.

"If you answer those questions over and over again, you can be successful dealing with people.

"The thing that I think is missing most in business is people who really understand how to deal with rank-and-file employees."

—Frederick W. Smith, founder, chairman,
and CEO, Federal Express

Mentoring is demeaning

"Mentoring as a whole is little more than one of those management popularities so beloved by consultants. From the perspective of the mentees, there is something demeaning about hitching their boat to an elegant cabin cruiser and being towed along in its wake. From the perspective of the mentor, there is a slight stench of injustice and hypocrisy in selecting a chosen few and lavishing time and attention on them. Any leader worthy of the name makes sure that _all_ people for whom they have responsibility have open and equitable opportunity to develop their abilities to the maximum."

—Dee Hock, founder and CEO,
Visa International

#20

A players hire A players, B players hire C players, and C players hire losers. Let your standards slip once and you're only two generations away from death.

Good people are in short supply

"Good people are in short supply. Whether you're an investor, a company owner, or someone strategically trying to figure out what to do in a business, you need to pay more attention to employee motivation and human relations."

—Esther Dyson, chairwoman,
EDventure Holdings

The unequal treatment of equals

"Nothing demotivates people like the equal treatment of unequals. When you hire a bozo and treat him the same as a rock star, it deflates the rock star."

—Joe Kraus, founder and CEO, JotSpot

Build on what they do best

"Don't try to change people. Instead, work to improve them."

—Doug Blevins, performance coach for
professional athletes

A never-ending journey

"A mentor has to make sure that the conversation around continuing development is inspiring, not intimidating. A great leader truly believes that personal development is a never-ending journey. If you can help people embrace and love continuous development, then you are really making a difference in their lives and careers."

—Betsey Bernard, former president, AT&T

You can't compromise

"You can't compromise on the people you use. You need to hire people who are confident and believe in what they do and can stand and face the wind when it blows hard."

—Joakim Jonason, creative director,
Cave Anhold Jonason

#21

If you lose great people, you lose success. It's that simple.

Stop trying to change people

"CEOs hate variance. It's the enemy. Variance in customer service is bad. Variance in quality is bad. CEOs love processes that are standardized, routinized, predictable. Stamping out variance makes a complex job a bit less complex.

"There is, however, one resource inside all companies that will hinder any attempt to eliminate variance: each individual's personality. You can't standardize human behavior. Of course, that's precisely what most leaders attempt to do. Standardizing human behavior is the driving force behind most executive-training programs and leadership-development courses. Not only is that approach psychologically daft, it's hugely inefficient. It's fighting human nature, and anyone who fights human nature will lose.

"The best managers don't even try to fight that fight. Instead, they follow the same basic set of principles: People don't change that much, so don't waste your time trying to rewire them or trying to put in what was left out. Instead, spend your time trying to draw out what was left in.

"When it comes to getting the best performance out of people, the most efficient route is to revel in their strengths, not to focus on their weaknesses."

—Marcus Buckingham and Curt Coffman,
authors, *First Break All the Rules*

Concentrate on the stars

"When it comes to training and performance reviews, I think we have our priorities reversed. Shouldn't we spend more time trying to improve the performance of our stars? After all, these people account for a disproportionately large share of the work in any organization. Put another way, concentrating on the stars is a highly leveraged activity; if they get better, the impact on group output is very large indeed."

—Andy Grove, chairman, Intel

Talent, talent, talent

"The difference between a good company and a great company is usually the talent level. If talent is a differentiating factor, you're going to have to reward that in order to keep it."

—David W. Dorman, chairman and CEO, AT&T

You're only as good as your people

"You're only as good as your people, that's why the war for talent is intense."

—Thomas Weisel, founder and CEO,
Thomas Weisel Partners

There are no limits

"There's absolutely no limit to what plain, ordinary people can accomplish if they are given the opportunity, encouragement and incentive to do their best."

—Sam Walton, founder, Wal-Mart

Understand what is behind every employee complaint

"Behind every employee complaint is an idea or a belief or a value that a person is committed to. Otherwise, why would they be upset? A person who complains that his boss is a jerk might be committed to the idea of having a relationship with that boss that is based on respect and trust."

—Lisa Laskow Lahey, professor,
Harvard University

Chemistry is important

"Chemistry is unbelievably important. If you come into a workplace and there is inconsistency, there are disruptive employees or you don't know what to expect, then you won't be a motivated employee."

—Pat Gillick, former general manager,
Seattle Mariners

If someone doesn't comply

"If someone doesn't comply with my wishes, I want to figure out why. I first look inward and ask myself three questions: Am I clearly articulating the goal? Am I giving that person enough training to accomplish the job? Am I giving that person enough time and tools to get the job done? When I don't get my desired result, I've found that 80 percent of the time the answer to one of those three questions provides me with a reason why."

—Mike Abrashoff, founder,
Grassroots Leadership

An invisible sign

"Everyone has an invisible sign around their neck that says, 'Make me feel important.' Never forget that when working with people."

—James B. Miller, entrepreneur and author,
The Corporate Coach

Invest in people

"If you want to empower people, invest in them. When you give people a loan, or you donate money to them, they're indebted to you. But when you invest in people, you demonstrate that you believe in them."

—E. David Ellington, co-founder, chairman,
CEO, and president, NetNoir

Give direction, not criticism

"Your job as a leader is to communicate a sense of how things could be—and to show people how to achieve that vision. How do you do all that? By giving direction, not criticism. Direction tells people what to do, whereas criticism tells people what not to do. Here's a criticism: 'The percussion section is playing too loudly.' A direction is, 'Make sure the audience can hear the woodwinds.'

"Direction points to the way things could be. Criticism, on the other hand, points to the way things were."

—Roger Nierenberg, conductor,
Stamford Symphony Orchestra

Concern costs nothing

"Turnover costs money. Concern costs nothing."

—James B. Miller, author, *The Corporate Coach*

Recruiting is everybody's job

"Everybody recruits at Dell. It's everybody's job. You can't just leave it to an HR organization. "

—Andy Esparza, vice president of talent
development and retention, Dell

Say thank you

"You can never thank people enough."

—Jeff Zucker, president, NBC Universal

ONE SIZE DOES *NOT* FIT ALL, BUT . . .

Clearly hiring, developing, and getting the best out of individual employees requires an approach that is slightly different for every one of your workers.

Still, there are some common rules you can apply in every situation:

- **Hire slow, fire fast.** You want to be absolutely sure you are hiring the best person. If that means rejecting people who could turn out to be stars, so be it. You can't run the risk of saying, "Maybe he'll work out." The damage an underperforming employee can do is tremendous. And if you make a mistake, cut your losses. Once it becomes clear that the person is not going to thrive, despite all your best efforts and coaching, you need to let them go.

- **If employees really are your most important asset,** you need to do everything in your power to make sure they are doing their best work. That means offering coaching, chances for development and promotion, and the best tools and work environment. Otherwise you are not using your most important asset to its fullest.

- **Having gone through the effort** required to achieve points one and two, you then must make sure your best employees stay. You keep the work challenging. You help them grow. You reward them fairly and

let them know that they are valued. Otherwise you
have wasted a lot of time, money, and effort—and
worse, you will lose your only source of competitive
advantage.

CHAPTER 9

Technology Is Not a Strategy

B ack when *Fast Company* started, we'd spend hour after hour interviewing CEOs, especially those in the high-tech industry, about their technology.

And we'd hear about how proprietary technology was, how hard it was to reverse-engineer, and why their hardware and software gave them an insurmountable competitive advantage.

We don't have those conversations anymore.

#22

Technology is *not* the answer. It can enable and support the corporate vision, but by itself, technology will *not* give you a competitive advantage.

The truth is that today just about everyone has access to the same technology. And if that is the case, technology can't give you a competitive edge.

In the case of technology, companies still need to be cutting-edge. But that has become the price of entry. Leaders today need to figure out how to do something with the technology that sets their company apart.

A lot of things follow from that—as you'll read throughout the chapter—but the biggest change is this: Information technology (IT) needs to be completely integrated into everything you do. Instead of keeping IT isolated from the rest of the company, the best firms link it both to overall corporate objectives and to the specific operating divisions it is designed to aid.

In other words, many leading firms have concluded that IT is too important to be left to the IT department.

Stripping the IT department of its virtual independence will not make you popular with chief information officers and the people who work for them, of course. But that is the price that smart leaders are willing to pay.

First, segregating any department from the rest of the company is inefficient. The natural tendency of departments set off by themselves is to look inward, focusing on their needs—"What is the coolest technology we could have?"—as opposed to looking outward—"What technology platform will let employees do the best job of taking care of our customers?"

Second, even with the price of computing steadily falling, the overall cost of IT, as a percentage of an organization's total operating budget, has been steadily increasing over the years as we find more and more ways technology can help us operate efficiently.

Anything that costs that much money should be both closely monitored and tied to the people and departments it is supposed to help.

The bottom line? IT is a tool—not a strategy.

The differentiator

"**The most meaningful way to differentiate your company from your competition, the best way to put distance between yourself and the crowd, is to do an outstanding job with information.** How you gather, manage, and use information will determine whether you win or lose."

—William H. Gates III, chairman,
Microsoft

#23

Operational silos are bad anywhere. But they are especially crippling when it comes to information technology (IT), which is vital to almost every organization's success.

Making something original

"Invention is to technology what conception is to reproduction—the moment that makes something original and unprecedented."

—Nathan P. Myhrvold, former chief
technology officer, Microsoft

Technology trends

"Here is something that might be reassuring if you are worried about missing out on a major technology trend. There has never been a technology breakthrough that changed everything overnight. Things don't change that quickly, and that is probably a good thing simply because people and corporations cannot absorb a lot of change quickly. It takes seven to 10 years for companies to come to grips with something completely new."

—Kevin O'Connor, founder of numerous companies including
DoubleClick, and author, *The Map of Innovation*

Reassembling knowledge

"Subjects like philosophy, history, and literature teach you how to interpret information and how to argue a point of view. That kind of sophisticated learning is a requirement for innovation and for entrepreneurship. Not only the written arts, but also music and the visual arts, will become increasingly important. Music, for example, teaches valuable lessons about time and space. Similarly, visual thinking is critical to using computers and to manipulating images across multiple dimensions.

"If we really want a society that can 'think different'—a goal that the high-tech world seems to applaud—then technology will not be the death knell of the humanities. Instead, humanities education will attract more attention. Original ideas come from reassembling knowledge in new ways. But you need to have that knowledge in your mind before you can reassemble it."

—Leon Botstein, president, Bard College

The servant of the people

"Technology should be the servant of the people. You have to believe in the majesty of the people. When you free people of the legitimate fear that technology is their executioner, then magical stuff can happen."

—Sidney Harman, chairman and CEO,
Harman International

Customer-driven

"For decades we all competed in what I would call an 'invent and assert' industry. We would create new technologies, and then we asserted—we projected and marketed—what we thought the technology could be used for. We have reached a point in our evolution where we can no longer be an industry driven by gizmos and guessing. We cannot grow this industry on that basis. Instead, we have to be driven by the needs of our clients."

—Samuel J. Palmisano, chairman and CEO, IBM

The CIO must take a leading role

"The CIO must take a real leading role as an enterprise executive, coaching and coaxing business colleagues about the potential business uses of particular technologies while also unlocking the information and business intelligence trapped inside business processes."

—Marianne Broadbent and Ellen Kitzis, authors,
The New CIO Leader: Setting the Agenda and Delivering Results

Why IT projects fail

"There are four key reasons why IT projects fail:
- The mandate given to the project team is vague and often contradictory.
- People with the necessary skills and knowledge are unavailable.
- The nature of the problems being worked on changes before the solution can be put into place.
- Senior management's input is hard to come by until it is too late."

—David Andrews and Kenneth Johnson, former CIOs
(at companies such as SmithKline and Timex)
turned consultants

Managing IT

"The CIO should have a front-row seat at all strategic-business planning discussions and advise on the role of technology. But the CIO should not make the final decisions about which technology investments make the most business sense."

—Mark Lutchen, author, Managing IT as a Business:
A Survival Guide for CEOs

IT is a commodity

"Information technology has increasingly become . . . a simple factor of production—a commodity input that is necessary for competitiveness, but insufficient for advantage."

—Nicholas G. Carr, former executive editor,
Harvard Business Review

FAST TAKE
THE CIO'S NEW ROLE

To: Chief information officers everywhere
From: The editors at *Fast Company*
Re: Your future

Your choice is as simple as it is stark: Do you want to leverage your expertise and take a larger and more strategic role within your company, or do you want to become a mechanic, someone whose sole job is just to make sure that the IT machinery works?

There is no middle ground, argue Marianne Broadbent, associate dean at the Melbourne Business School, and Ellen Kitzis, group vice president of the Gartner consulting firm's executive programs.

It is easy to understand how CIOs have gotten to this crossroad. There is a growing dissatisfaction with IT caused by the Internet bust, the overexpenditure on technology capacity, and the growing (and correct) belief that technology itself cannot be a form of competitive advantage.

As a result, some senior managers want to downplay the IT function, turning the CIO, in the words of Broadbent and Kitzis, into "the chief technology mechanic, a role ultimately no more prestigious than that of the factory floor manager."

Can CIOs avoid this diminution?

Yes, Broadbent and Kitzis contend. Clever CIOs can reposition themselves to become the focal point of everything the company does.

The key is to make sure that two things are true of the IT department:

1. It functions as efficiently as possible, delivering cost-effective services.
2. It is best positioned to help the company build on its competitive advantage.

The pressure on CIOs to justify their budgets is only going to steadily increase going forward. CIOs will need to figure out a good answer to the question "Why should we give your department so much money?" Otherwise, they may very well be relegated to the role of chief mechanic.

CHAPTER 10
Knowledge

Management fads come and go.

#24

Don't have your people waste time figuring out what someone else in the company has already discovered. Create and maintain an efficient knowledge management system to share experiences companywide.

But there is one fashionable idea that came and went that we would like to bring back: knowledge management, sometimes referred to as managing intellectual capital.

No matter what you call it, the idea became all the rage

back at the tail end of the 1980s and into the very early 1990s. The idea, which struck us as worthwhile then, is compelling now: You figure out a way to capture everything your organization knows, and then create an easy way for everyone in the company to access that knowledge.

For example, you compile a database of the best practices you have undertaken for specific clients, and next time a similar assignment comes up, employees can see what approach worked well in the past.

There is a lot to be gained by capturing this sort of institutional knowledge. By some estimates, up to 70 percent of what workers do is nothing more than reinventing a wheel that their organization had discovered earlier.

You can waste inordinate amounts of time, energy, and resources having your employees learn on their own what your company already knows. And with the competition being what it is today, these are resources you can't afford to waste.

It's vital for you to find ways to ensure that everything your organization knows is accessible to everyone in your organization.

Knowledge management

"Knowledge is a fluid mix of framed experience, values, contextual information, and expert insight that provides a framework for evaluating and incorporating new experiences and information. It originates and is applied in the minds of the knowers. In organizations, it often becomes embedded not only in documents but also in organizational routines, processes, practices and norms."

—Thomas H. Davenport and Laurence Prusak,
authors, *Working Knowledge*

You are competing based on the knowledge of your employees

"Knowledge management is really about recognizing that regardless of what business you are in, you are competing based on the knowledge of your employees."

—Cindy Johnson, director of collaboration
and knowledge sharing, Texas Instruments

It may sound silly, but . . .

"If you think the name 'knowledge management' sounds silly, relax. No one else likes this name either. . . .

"The sticking point is the word 'management.' It evokes an image of someone in a business suit . . . reaching into people's brains for knowledge, rifling through the contents, and somehow managing the knowledge found there as easily as if it were auto parts. . . .

"Many specialists in the field shudder at the term 'knowledge management' because it fails to name even one of the activities associated with knowledge—creating, identifying, sharing, capturing, acquiring, and leveraging knowledge, to name a few. But at this point the name has become so well known that we're stuck with it."

—Melissie Clemmons Rumizen, author,
The Complete Idiot's Guide to Knowledge Management

Everything can be traced back to the same source

"In the end, the location of the . . . economy is not in the technology, be it the microchip or the global communication network. It is in the human mind."

—Alan M. Webber, co-founder, *Fast Company*

Take time to reflect

"It's hard to share knowledge if you don't have enough time to reflect on what you know or what you need to learn. Most companies have squeezed almost all of the reflection time out of their business processes. People don't have the time to think about what they're going to do next, let alone who they should talk to about it."

—John Old, knowledge manager, Texaco

Best practices

"Best practices usually aren't."

—Christopher Locke, co-author, *The Cluetrain Manifesto*

Where are our assets?

"The inventory goes down the elevator every night."

—Fairfax Cone, advertising executive

#25

Data are a series of facts. Information is a lot of data about a topic combined with some context. Ideally companies want to manage information in such a way that it yields knowledge: information that has been processed in such a way that it can be used for competitive advantage.

Translating experience into knowledge

"Translating experience into knowledge may seem like something that happens automatically in an organization, but unfortunately it does not. Remember the old joke about the teacher who rather than having twenty years of teaching experience had the same experience twenty times? We all probably know a few people like that. In fact, it takes a certain amount of intention to create knowledge out of an experience."

—Nancy M. Dixon, author, *Common Knowledge:*
How Companies Thrive by Sharing What They Know

Putting knowledge to work

"A good strategy must not only account for an organization's tacit knowledge, but also channel it wisely."

—Georg Von Krogh, author, *Enabling Knowledge Creation*

Competing in the global economy

"Managing knowledge is something all companies will have to master if they expect to compete in a global economy. Those that can learn quickly and then leverage and use that knowledge within the company will have a big advantage over those that can't."

Ken Derr, former CEO, Chevron

20 percent

"No executive would leave his cash or factory space idle, yet if CEOs are asked how much of the knowledge in their companies is used, they typically say, 'About 20 percent.'"

—Thomas A. Stewart, editor, *Harvard Business Review,*
and author, *Intellectual Capital*

Knowledge is an infinite resource

"Variously referred to as intellectual capital, intellectual property, knowledge assets, or business intelligence, corporate knowledge is now being viewed as the last and only sustainable untapped source of competitive advantage in business. Unlike other forms of capital—land, equipment, labor, and money—knowledge is theoretically infinite. There's always a new idea waiting to be discovered: new ways of doing things, new strategies, new products, new markets."

—Mark W. McElroy, author, *The New Knowledge Management:*
Complexity, Learning, and Sustainable Innovation

The only new thing

"The only thing new in the world is the history you don't know."

—President Harry S Truman

Companies back up their data every night. But what are they doing to save their organization's institutional knowledge?

Probably not much.

David W. DeLong, a research fellow at MIT's AgeLab and an adjunct professor at Babson College, says that is especially troubling because members of the largest generation ever to work—baby boomers—have already started to retire.

Most companies, he says, are simply not prepared for the fact that a significant portion of what those workers know—knowledge that has never been captured anywhere—will be walking out the door with them once they leave the workforce.

Of course, knowledge disappearing has been a problem throughout time. Just think of the lost Library of Alexandria or the fact that no one knows how Stradivarius made a violin.

But what makes the problem more severe today, says DeLong, is that the knowledge we are about to lose is more complex, more abstract, and more costly to re-create than ever before.

To eliminate the problem, he proposes multiple solutions—everything from staggering retirements, so that companies don't get hit hard all at once, to formal processes in which retiring employees are in essence debriefed so that remaining workers can capture what they know.

What might those processes look like? Dorothy Leonard,

a retired Harvard Business School professor, and Walter Swap, a former professor at Tufts, have some helpful ideas.

First, someone determines what information needs to be transferred.

Next, you need someone to do the transferring; Leonard and Swap refer to this person as a "knowledge coach." The knowledge coach makes sure all information is transferred and that it is going to the right person, someone who not only can benefit from it but wants to possess it.

Finally, the coach checks to see that the knowledge that was transferred was actually understood. She does that by having the receiver put it to use in real-life situations.

This is an important subject. As a matter of course, companies back up their data. They should be backing up their institutional knowledge as well. If you are not capturing that know-how in a formal way, you should be.

CHAPTER 11

Leadership

Malcolm S. Forbes, Sr., the man who turned his father's small investment publication into a international business magazine, gave what may be the best one-sentence description of leadership we have ever heard, and he did it with an incredibly simple analogy.

At lunch one day, a young investor looking for tips asked him: "How can you truly know whether a company is going to be successful?"

#26

The principles governing how you lead must remain absolutely constant. How you express them must vary every single time, depending on your audience. *You* need to make sure they understand what you are trying to do—and what their role is.

"You bet on the jockey," said Forbes. "Not the horse."

He is absolutely right. You have to bet on the chief executive officer (the jockey) because any business (the horse) is always in a constant state of flux. New companies enter the fray. A radical shift in technology changes the competitive landscape. A new opportunity suddenly appears. Interest rates suddenly rise (or fall). Mergers and acquisitions radically change the sector. The list is endless.

Investors (and employees) count on the person at the top to make the right decisions in response. That person sets the vision, makes sure it is followed out, and lives the values he wants his company to represent. Said that way, leadership sounds remarkably simple. As you know from real life, it is not.

Still, the best leaders have learned—often the hard way—tactics and approaches that can increase the odds of being successful, as you'll find here.

Changing minds

"Leaders are almost by definition people who change minds."

—Howard Gardner, professor, Harvard University, and author, *Leading Minds*

To be a leader

"To be a leader is to be awake and alert, to be dissatisfied at all times."

—Peter Koestenbaum, philosophy professor turned consultant

The difference between leaders and managers

"The manager administers; the leader innovates.

The manager is a copy; the leader is an original.

The manager maintains; the leader develops.

The manager accepts reality; the leader investigates it.

The manager focuses on systems and structure; the leader focuses on people.

The manager relies on control; the leader inspires trust.

The manager has a short-term view; the leader has a long-range perspective.

The manager asks how and when; the leader asks what and why.

The manager has her eye always on the bottom line; the leader has her eye on the horizon.

The manager imitates; the leader originates.

The manager accepts the status quo; the leader challenges it.

The manager is the classic good soldier; the leader is her own person.

The manager does things right; the leader does the right thing."

—Warren Bennis, professor, University of Southern California, and author, *Learning to Lead*, and Joan Goldsmith

Emotional and intellectual anchors

"When the going is toughest, leaders must behave like emotional and intellectual anchors. The critical issues are about faith, passion and most importantly, authenticity. People must know you are not pretending. They can see a sham."

—C. K. Prahalad, professor, University of Michigan

What I learned at West Point

"The first lesson I learned as a plebe came from an upper-classman yelling in my face. He told me that there were four acceptable answers: 'Yes, sir'; 'No, sir'; 'No excuse, sir'; and 'Sir, I do not understand.' He'd ask, 'Why aren't your shoes shined?' and I'd say, 'Well, it was muddy, and I didn't have time.' He'd be all over me. He was trying to teach me something: If you have to take men up a hill and write letters to [the mothers of the men who did not make it back down] that night, there's literally no excuse. If you have to lay off thousands of people from your company, there's no excuse. You should have seen it coming and done something about it."

—James Kimsey, founding CEO,
America Online

The people in the trenches

"The people at the so-called bottom of an organization know more about what's going on than the people at the top. The people in the trenches are the ones in the best position to make critical decisions. It's up to leaders to give those people the freedom and the resources that they need."

—Martin Sorrell, CEO, WPP Group

A noble cause

"Building an enduring great company—one that is truly worthy of lasting—is a noble cause."

—Jim Collins, author, *Good to Great*

You can't create a leader in a classroom

"We are creating a business class that believes it has the right to lead because it spent a couple of years in the classroom. You can't create a leader in a classroom."

—Henry Mintzberg, professor of management,
McGill University

Roll up your sleeves

"Believe me, any time a boss will roll up his or her sleeves and actually do some grunt work, word will reach every corner of the shop."

—Harvey Mackay, author,
Swim with the Sharks

If you go broke, you can't take care of anyone

"As company leaders, we have a fiduciary duty to the people we work with. We need to make our businesses successful, and that means profitable.

"People come to work to improve the quality of their life, for themselves and for their family. If they are willing to do excellent work, then as the people running companies, we must help them achieve their goals, and the only way that is going to happen is if we keep our companies in business. And to stay in business, our companies must make a profit. (Besides, from the customers' point of view, you can't give good service if you go bankrupt.)"

—Carl Sewell, the most successful luxury
car dealer in the United States

 # 27

Leaders lead.

Toxic leaders

"Leaders who cannot confront their own mistakes are probably not leaders we can trust."

—Jean Lipman-Blumen, author,
The Allure of Toxic Leaders

Your power is in your people

"All your power is in your people. Your job is enabling everybody to contribute to their fullest."

—Alan R. Mulally, executive vice president,
Boeing

Persuasion, conciliation, and patience

"I happen to know a little about leadership. And I tell you this: You do not lead by hitting people over the head. Any damn fool can do that, but it's usually called 'assault,' not 'leadership.'

"I'll tell you what leadership is. It's persuasion, and conciliation, and patience. It's long, slow, tough work. That's the only sort of leadership I know or believe in—or will practice."

—President Dwight D. Eisenhower

Tyranny

"If you don't understand that you work for your mislabeled 'subordinates,' then you know nothing about leadership. You know only tyranny."

—Dee Hock, founder and CEO emeritus,
Visa International

#28

Leadership is the art of getting people to do what *you* want because *they* want to.

The CEO is not Superman

"There is a certain mythology right now in the world that thinks the CEO is a kind of superman. But in fact, business is so darn complicated, and the decisions are so important, there is no one person alone who is going to be maximally effective in making those decisions."

—Kevin Sharer, chairman and CEO, Amgen

Truly caring

"The most important thing in good leadership is truly caring. The best people in any profession care about the people they lead, and the people who are being led know when it's faked or not there at all."

—Dean Smith, Hall of Fame basketball coach

What leaders don't do

"Here's what leaders don't do. They don't blame underlings. They don't blame their predecessor. They don't complain about press coverage. They don't whine about Wall Street. They don't mindlessly cut research and development. They don't fire 4,000 people in the hope that it will bump up their company's stock for the weekend. They don't obfuscate, dissemble or lie. They don't hide behind a retinue of handlers and lawyers and public relations fools."

—John Ellis, media consultant

Well thought out

"Well thought out demands mobilize effort, and establish a sense of control of a work program. When you have thought through what needs to be done, and have called on the right people to do it in the right way, everyone involved comes away with an 'up' feeling. The recipients have a clear sense of their responsibilities, tasks and timetables for action. If assignments are shared and mutually understood among members of a management team, people have a greater sense of coordinated action toward a goal."

—Robert A. Neiman, author, *Execution Plain and Simple*

Simplify

"The role of a leader is to simplify. Knowledge work is all about how we use one another's time and attention. Given just minutes, good leaders can affect how we think, what we decide and ultimately what we create."

—Bill Jensen, author, *What Is Your Life's Work?*

Listening to the voice of David

"When you seek out junior voices, two things surprise you: how much those young [people] have to say and how important it is. I've learned that lesson multiple times during my career and it is about listening to what I call 'the voice of David.' It's actually a tradition in Benedictine monasteries. When a decision has to be made, the abbot asks each monk's opinion, starting with the youngest. The order is intentional. In the Bible, nobody listens to David. There were plenty of gizmos with which to fight Goliath, and David was dismissed as a punk kid with a slingshot. In the end, the kid was right. When I've made a good decision, it's usually because I've listened to the voice of David. And when I made a poor decision, I haven't taken the time to listen."

—Patrick T. Harker, dean, Wharton School of Business,
University of Pennsylvania

Be curious

"Good leaders are very curious; they spend a lot of time trying to learn new things."

—Jeffrey Immelt, CEO, General Electric

The primal job of leadership is emotional

"The fundamental task of leaders . . . is to prime good feeling in those they lead. That occurs when a leader creates resonance—a reservoir of positivity that unleashes the best in people. At its root, then, the primal job of leadership is emotional."

—Daniel Goleman, Richard Boyatzis, and Annie McKee,
authors, *Primal Leadership*

Vision

"Leadership is about making a vision happen."

—Lorraine Monroe, founder and executive director,
The School Leadership Academy

Give direction

"If you expect those below to support your leadership and step into the breach when needed, they will need to understand your strategy, your methods, and your rules. That requires repeated restatements of your principles and consistent adherence to them."

—Michael Useem, professor, University of Pennsylvania,
and author, *Leading Up*

Growing your people

"The most important job you have is growing your people, giving them a chance to reach their dreams."

—Jack Welch, former chairman and CEO of GE
and author, *Winning*

#29

Leaders need to say two things: "This is where we are going," and "This is why we need you to help us get there."

Servant leadership

"I'm a big believer in servant leadership. A leader's job is to serve the staff."

—Dan Cathy, president and COO, Chick-fil-A

The challenges of leadership

"Recognizing the challenges of leadership, along with the pains of change, shouldn't diminish anyone's eagerness to reap the rewards of creating value and meaning in other people's lives. There's a thrill that comes with the creation of value—and of course there's money and status—and those rewards are surely worth the pain that comes with the territory. There are lots of things in life that are worth the pain. Leadership is one of them."

—Ronald Heifetz, lecturer, Harvard Business School

Leadership is about responsibility

"By leadership I mean taking complete responsibility for an organization's well-being and growth and changing it for the better. Real leadership is not about prestige, power, or status. It is about responsibility."

—Robert L. Joss, dean, Stanford
Graduate School of Business

Teaching

"I don't know if teaching is my number one job, but it's pretty close."

—Craig E. Weatherup, former chairman and CEO,
Pepsi Bottling Group

Focus

"You can't do everything. Focus on what will make the biggest impact. Communicate your goals relentlessly so that everyone else knows what their own focus should be."

—Bonnie Reitz, former senior vice president,
Continental Airlines

Leaders develop other leaders

"If you're a leader, the idea is to help others learn, to help each person become fully in charge. You don't do that by preaching at people or yelling at them. We help them get it for themselves."

—Suzanne Pogell, founder and president, Womanship,
a sailing school in Annapolis, Maryland

Say thank you

"The first responsibility of a leader is to define reality. The last is to say thank you."

—Max DePree, former chairman and CEO of
Herman Miller, author, *Leadership Is an Art*

FAST TAKE
HOW TO LEAD

Why do the best leaders succeed? There seem to be five constants when you look at why the best leaders succeed.

They know where they want to go. The best leaders are extremely clear about what the future for their company needs to look like. Equally important, they have a definitive road map for getting their company to where they want it to be.

They know who is going to help them get there. They are extremely careful in their hiring and in whom they promote.

They make sure those people understand—and have bought into—that vision.

They make sure those people have the tools—training and technology—to accomplish the vision.

They give constant feedback, giving coaching where needed, and changing personnel as necessary.

CHAPTER 12

Life and Career

W ork is personal.

There truly is no way to separate what you do from who you are. Of course we are all more than what we do for a living, but work is so integral to our lives that it is silly to pretend we can draw an arbitrary line that neatly separates our lives into two parts—work and nonwork.

#30

Achieving balance in your life is a time-management problem and needs to be treated as such. What that means is you figure out what you absolutely must accomplish in your personal and professional lives, and let everything else slide.

Since that arbitrary division doesn't fly, we need something that will. Each of us needs to find out exactly how much space we want work to take up in our lives.

Each of us has only one life to live. You need to figure out how you want to live it.

What should I do with my life

"Addressing the question, What should I do with my life? . . . [is] a moral imperative. It's how we hold ourselves accountable to the opportunity we're given. Most of us are blessed with the ultimate privilege: We get to be true to our individual nature. Our economy is so vast that we don't have to grind it out forever at jobs we hate. For the most part, we get to choose. That choice isn't about a career search so much as an identity quest. Asking The Question aspires to end the conflict between who you are and what you do. There is nothing more brave than filtering out the chatter that tells you to be someone you're not. There is nothing more genuine than breaking away from the chorus to learn the sound of your own voice. Asking The Question is nothing short of an act of courage: It requires a level of commitment and clarity that is almost foreign to our working lives."

—Po Bronson, author, *What Should I Do with My Life?*

Only you can stop you

"Others can stop you temporarily—you are the only one who can do it permanently."

—Zig Ziglar, founder and CEO, Ziglar Training Systems,
and author, *See You at the Top*

Balance

"People who have learned to answer email on Sunday evenings also need to learn how to go to the movies on Monday afternoons. By redesigning the architecture of time, we can make room for work, leisure and idleness. All three can coexist and harmonize together to produce happiness and a sense of purpose."

—Ricardo Sempler, president, Semco

#31

You can do anything, but not everything.

Finding job satisfaction in the work itself

"You must find job satisfaction in the work itself. Your self-esteem must come from doing the work rather than from some hoped-for promotion, pay raise, or other reward—which may never materialize."

—Richard Bolles, author,
What Color Is Your Parachute?

How to build your career

"Do not underestimate the power of the brand you're associated with. Go blue chip earlier in your career. It's like going to a great university. It's great taking entrepreneurial risk, but you have to establish a track record at one of these recognizable companies first."

—James M. Citrin, executive recruiter,
Spencer Stuart

Be a spin doctor

"Yes, you have your story of what you've done in your job, but you have to put the best twist on it. On each gig, you must be marketing your worth, marketing Me Inc. You can go too far (think Dennis Kozlowski or Martha Stewart), but you constantly have to spin-doctor. If you don't, you have what I call the 'engineer's mentality'—and I am an engineer by training. People with an engineer's mentality believe that truth and virtue will automatically be their own reward. That's a crock."

—Tom Peters, co-author,
In Search of Excellence

Love what you do

"What advice would I give my grandchildren? That's the easiest question in the world. Do something you enjoy—music, business, public service, whatever. If you don't enjoy going to work, I don't care if your IQ is 30 points higher than the other guy's, the guy with the inferior IQ—who loves what he is doing—will beat you to death every time."

—Ace Greenberg, chairman of executive
committee, Bear Stearns

Do what you love

"Do what you love, the money will follow."

—Marsha Sinetar, author,
Do What You Love, the Money Will Follow

More than a job

"Remember you are more than your job."

—Ronald A. Heifetz and Marty Linsky,
professors, Harvard University

Think about what is worthwhile

"You only have so many seconds of attention to give to your work and to your personal life. Think seriously about what you think is worthwhile, what isn't, and what difference it all makes. . . . We live in a browsing society that focuses on the shallowest, most hype-oriented aspects of life. Nobody goes deeply into any topic. It's bound to mean that we're not making the best decisions in the areas that matter most to us."

—Thomas H. Davenport, fellow, Institute for
Higher-Performance Business, Accenture

Lateral moves

"Don't minimize the importance of lateral moves and broad development. I did a number of lateral moves in my career, and not only did it not hurt me, it actually helped tremendously. I feel like I've got a good operational grounding in most aspects of our business. At some point in my 25 years of working, I've touched very closely or led most of the functions we have here in [the organization]. That's been exceptionally valuable."

—Myrtle S. Potter, president,
commercial operations, Genentech

Keep looking

"If you're not passionate about what you do, keep looking. I found my passion very early in life and that's all I've ever done."

—Julia Stewart, chief executive officer, IHOP

#32

Take breaks. Not only will it make you more productive, if you go out and see the world you are bound to spot opportunities.

Suck it up

"I've got three words for you: Suck it up. Intense psychotherapy and pharmaceuticals might have a significant impact on your boss's behavior—but you won't. It's not up to you to change your boss, but you can change your situation. You can do this in one of three ways: impose or relax constraints on the situation, work your way around the situation, or get out of the situation."

—Leonard A. Schlesinger, COO,
Limited Brands

The Golden Rule

"Do unto others as you would have others do unto you."

—Just about every religion in the world

The 7 habits of highly effective people

Who are we to argue?

More than 15 million people have bought a copy of *The 7 Habits of Highly Effective People*, by Stephen R. Covey, so there may be something there.

The seven habits?

1. "Be proactive."
2. "Begin with the end in mind."
3. "Put first things first."
4. "Think win-win."
5. "Seek first to understand, then to be understood."
6. "Synergize."
7. "Sharpen the saw" (engage in personal renewal).

The 8th habit

"Voice . . . lies at the nexus of *talent* (your natural gifts and strengths), *passion* (those things that naturally energize, excite, motivate and inspire you), *need* (including what the world needs enough to pay you for), and *conscience* (that still, small voice within that assures you of what is right and that prompts you to actually do it)."

—Stephen R. Covey, author, *The 8th Habit*

Every second counts

"When it comes to time management, I have one piece of advice: Push yourself as hard as you can. Always push yourself, even when it hurts—because every second counts."

—Todd Krizelman, co-CEO, theglobe.com

Unhappy bedfellows

"Humans are creative, fun and inquiring; yet work for so many is monotonous, complex, and dreary.

"Humans are individual and versatile; yet at work we discover we are all expendable and carefully placed in a well-mannered organogram.

"I'm not at all surprised that Homo sapiens and Work are unhappy bedfellows. The average corporation lives half as long as the average human, which means that most of us will have been part of a company that is thrashing around in its death throes at some stage in our lives."

—Andy Law, author, Creative Company

You own your career

"Jobs are given and jobs are taken away—often by forces you can't control. But your career belongs to you."

—Eunice Azzani, managing director,
Korn/Ferry International

Grow your own idea

"There's nothing more appealing than someone who wants to try to grow their own idea."

—Gary Cowger, president, North American
operations, General Motors

The things that matter most

"Do the things that matter most to you. If you don't love it, it's not worth it."

—Dan Rosensweig, chief operating officer, Yahoo

Passing through the fire

"We learn . . . by growing older, by suffering, by loving, by bearing with the things we can't change, by taking risks.

"The things you learn in maturity are not simple things such as acquiring information and skills. . . . You learn not to engage in self-destructive behavior. You learn not to burn up energy in anxiety. You learn to manage your tensions, if you have any, which you do. You learn that self-pity and resentment are among the most toxic of drugs. You learn that the world loves talent but pays off on character.

"You learn that most people are neither for you nor against you: they are thinking about themselves. You learn that no matter how much you strive to please, there are some people in this world who are not going to love you, a lesson that is at first troubling and then really quite relaxing. . . .

"Those are things that are hard to learn early in life. As a rule you have to have picked up some mileage and some dents in your fenders before you understand. As Norman Douglas said, 'There are some things you can't learn from others. You have to pass through the fire."

—John W. Gardner, former president,
Carnegie Corporation, and founder, Common Cause

Balance is bunk

"Balance is bunk. It is an unattainable pipe dream, a vain artifice that offers mostly rhetorical solutions to problems of logistics and economics."

—Keith Hammonds, deputy editor, *Fast Company*

Looking smart

"Remind people that profit is the difference between revenue and expense. This makes you look smart."

—Scott Adams, business commentator and
creator of Dilbert

Your inner voice

"It's important to have a deep inner life, to think about the important things, like spirituality, and ponder what life is all about. Without it, I think you respond too much to external voices instead of listening to your own inner voice."

—Bill George, former CEO, Medtronic

No entitlements

"One of the most pervasive myths in the American culture today is that we are entitled to a great life—that somehow, somewhere, someone (certainly not us) is responsible for filling our lives with continual happiness, exciting career options, nurturing family time, and blissful personal relationships simply because we exist.

"But the real truth ... is there is only one person responsible for the quality of the life you live.

"That person is you.

"If you want to be successful, you have to take 100% responsibility for everything that you experience in your life."

—Jack Canfield, author,
The Success Principles

FAST TAKE
TIME, TIME, TIME IS ON YOUR SIDE (YES IT IS)

The only way you are going to be more productive is if you decide you really want to be more productive.

As intuitive as that sounds, most people—especially executives—don't, argue Heike Bruch, a professor of leadership at the University of St. Gallen in Switzerland, and Sumantra Ghoshal, a London Business School professor.

After surveying executives across a number of industries, the authors came to the depressing conclusion that only 10 percent of managers are particularly good at getting things done. The rest, the professors argue, confuse action with accomplishment.

The secret to getting things done, the authors conclude, is to have willpower (energy plus focus) and to set a goal and stick to it.

Where do you apply all that determination?

All the time-management experts offer what boils down to the same advice: Focus on simplifying your life. In other words, concentrate on what is truly important to you and eliminate the rest. To oversimplify, if your goal is to learn how to play the piano, you could free up some time to practice by forgetting about painting the inside of all your closets.

With that as your strategy, here are some tactics to get more done:

- Match projects to your energy cycles. Most people have more pep at different parts of the day. Leave the easy stuff for the times when you traditionally feel sluggish.

- If you work at home and neighbors are constantly stopping by, come to the door holding a phone to your ear (whether or not someone is on the other end) and mouth to your neighbor that you will call them later.

- At work, ask yourself this: "If I stopped doing X, would anybody actually notice?" If not, you just freed up some time.

- Not only back up all the material on your computer—so that you are prepared for the inevitable crash—but rid it of unwanted files and programs so that it will run faster.

- To cut down on idle chit-chat that can waste time, return phone calls when you know the other person isn't in, leaving a detailed message on their voice mail.

- If you tell someone you are going to follow up, tell the person when you are going to do it and then do it. It eliminates all those "when are you going to follow up?" calls and e-mails.

- If you want to reduce the clutter in your e-mail in-box, get yourself taken off every single routing list where you are not vital.

Perhaps the most intriguing thing to note is this: Successful executives don't view the constant interruptions in their days as disruptions but rather a chance to learn what is going on, coach, and manage.

Years ago, this concept was called "managing by wandering around." Today, it is probably best described as managing by having people come to you.

CHAPTER 13
Managing

I f you have ever served in the military, or even seen a movie set on a military base, you will recognize this scene.

A young recruit—one who was initially as anti-military as you could get and is now trying desperately to become the best soldier in the armed services—has just been chewed out by a grizzled noncommissioned officer, maybe a master sergeant. The bewildered recruit, trying to make amends, says, "I'm sorry, sir."

That just makes the sergeant even madder.

"Sir? Don't call me sir," the sergeant screams, inches from the recruit's face. "Do I look like an officer to you? I work for a living."

We have always pictured managers, everyone from plant managers up to and including senior vice presidents, as noncommissioned officers—the master sergeants, the leaders who actually work for a living.

Leaders may determine the overarching vision and strategy, but it is up to managers to get the actual work done.

#33

Great managers are just as important as great leaders.

Survey after survey has shown that managers hold the key to employee engagement. If employees have a good relationship with their immediate boss, they work harder and stay committed to the organization. If they don't, they won't.

Add up those two factors—managers are the people who make sure the work gets done, and they are primarily responsible for whether employees perform at peak levels and stay with the company—and it is easy to see why they are a vital part of any organization's success.

The best people you can find

"Surround yourself with the best people you can find, delegate authority, and don't interfere as long as the policy you've decided upon is being carried out."

—President Ronald Reagan

The art of human relationships

"Here is one of the best bits of advice ever given about the fine art of human relationships: 'If there is any one secret of success,' said Henry Ford, 'it lies in the ability to get the other person's point of view and see things from that angle as well as your own.' . . .

"That is so simple, so obvious, that anyone ought to see the truth of it at a glance, yet 90 percent of the people on this earth ignore it 90 percent of the time."

—Dale Carnegie, author, *How to Win Friends and Influence People*

Manage, don't lead

"There's not a lot of room anymore for senior people to be managers. They have to be leaders."

—Anne M. Mulcahy, Chairman
and CEO, Xerox Corp.

The flywheel effect

"Picture a huge, heavy flywheel. It's a massive, metal disk mounted horizontally on an axle. It's about 100 feet in diameter, 10 feet thick, and it weighs about 25 tons. That flywheel is your company. Your job is to get that flywheel to move as fast as possible, because momentum—mass times velocity—is what will generate superior economic results over time.

"Right now, the flywheel is at a standstill. To get it moving, you . . . push with all of your might, and finally, you get the flywheel to inch forward. After two or three days of sustained effort, you get the flywheel to complete one entire turn. You keep pushing, and the flywheel begins to move a bit faster. It takes a lot of work, but at last the flywheel makes a second rotation. You keep pushing steadily. It makes three turns, four turns, five, six. With each turn, it moves faster, and then—at some point, you can't say exactly when—you break through. The momentum of the heavy wheel kicks in your favor. It spins faster and faster, with its own weight propelling it. You aren't pushing any harder, but the flywheel is accelerating, its momentum building, its speed increasing.

"This is the Flywheel Effect. It's what it feels like when you're inside a company that makes the transition from good to great."

—Jim Collins, author, *Good to Great*

Confidence

"Don't let them see you sweat. Have confidence in your ability."

—Loren B. Belker, author, *The First-time Manager*

The empowering manager

"The empowering leader creates the best possible conditions for performance and career development. The message sounds like this: 'I believe in you, your judgment, capabilities, and your potential. I expect you to be successful. I am here to aid you, to act as a catalyst for your success. My job is to create the conditions for your success; your job is to get it done. We will work on it together.'"

—Edward H. Betof, author, *Just Promoted: How to Survive and Thrive in Your First 12 Months as a Manager*

#34

The closer top management is to the customer, the more successful an organization is likely to be.

Recognition

"What we recognize in others helps them shape their identity and their future accomplishments."

—Tom Rath and Donald O. Clifton, authors, *How Full Is Your Bucket? Positive Strategies for Work and Life*

What gets done

"What gets measured gets done."

—Peter F. Drucker, management icon

How to be a great coach

"It's easy to be a great coach when you have great players."

—Michael McNeal, former director of corporate
employment, Cisco Systems

Put down the whip

"You don't have to beat the horse to run faster. We quit whipping the horse, and things improved."

—Gordon Bethune, chairman and CEO,
Continental Airlines

People who feel good about themselves

"People who feel good about themselves produce good results."

—Kenneth Blanchard, author,
The One Minute Manager

If the line manager is not innovating

"If the line manager is not innovating, then innovation is not going to occur."

—Peter Senge, author, *The Fifth Discipline*

The right to make mistakes

"Developing people means improving their current skills, teaching them new skills, helping them eliminate weaknesses, increasing their responsibilities, and moving them to new assignments to broaden their experience. It also means delegating appropriate decision-making and implementing authority to them. That includes the right to make some mistakes and learn from them. . . .

"The best person to practice on is yourself because the most difficult person to properly manage and to develop is yourself."

—Robert W. Gallant, author, *How to Be a Manager*

Tired ears

"There's a marvelous Middle Eastern phrase about leaders who've stopped listening. They say, 'He has tired ears.' That's arrogance."

—Warren Bennis, professor, U.S.C.

Face the problem head-on

"I've had a lot of experience turning around troubled companies, and one of the first things I learned was that whatever hard or painful things you have to do, do them quickly and make sure everyone knows what you are doing and why. Whether dwelling on a problem, hiding a problem, or dribbling out partial solutions to a problem while you wait for a high tide to raise your boat—dithering and delay almost always compound a negative situation. I believe in getting the problem behind me quickly and moving on."

—Louis V. Gerstner, Jr., former chairman
and CEO, IBM

Why managers are failing

"Today's workers are different than the metalworker/blue-collar employees who dominated our economy when most management techniques were developed. Today's knowledge workers are more specialized and they have more skills and as a result more choices. They will not stand for raw power. You can't lead them by bullying. They need information. Persuasion. And they need their leaders to listen to them."

—Ram Charan, consultant and co-author, *Execution*

#35

Your employees are never going to know how they are doing—and how they can do better—unless you tell them.

The long-term good

"If a crisis occurs, the company must act fast, be honest, and keep customers and the general public informed. Today, it is no longer realistic to believe that the truth will never come out or that financial damage can be postponed indefinitely, so attempting to cover up a debacle may result in greater reputational damage to the company than openly admitting any mistakes that have been made. The company's response should focus on its long-term good, rather than on minimizing immediate losses."

—James Lam, author, *Enterprise Risk Management*

Managers must juggle

"Managers must juggle diverse, often ambiguous, responsibilities and are enmeshed in a web of relationships with people who often make conflicting demands: subordinates, bosses, and others inside and outside the organization. As a result, the daily routine in management is often pressured, hectic, and fragmented."

—Linda A. Hill, author, *Becoming a Manager:*
How New Managers Master the Challenges of Leadership

It's nice if they like you, but . . .

"If your goal is to get everyone to like you, you will avoid making tough decisions because of fear of upsetting your 'friends.'"

—David Cottrell, author, *Monday Morning Leadership*

Weak managers never say, "I don't know"

"Weak managers never say these three words: 'I don't know.' Instead they respond, 'Let me get back to you on that,' and waste half a day trying to ferret out the answer in order to save face. Others opt for condescension and say, 'I think the information will be more meaningful to you if you dig it out for yourself.' Still others simply lie and hope their best guesses are correct. . . .

"When we dodge issues, or duck the facts, when we pretend to know more than we do, we demonstrate a lack of emotional maturity, something that any leader greatly needs."

—W. Steven Brown, author, *13 Fatal Errors*
Managers Make and How You Can Avoid Them

FAST TAKE
ENGAGING WITH EMPLOYEES

More than the paycheck, colleagues, or working conditions, it is the manager who has the greatest effect on whether an employee is happy and productive—or not. Nothing else comes close. So forging a relationship with the people who work for you is vital.

But not every manager is naturally good at doing that. For those of us who need help building relationships with employees, the authors of *How Full Is Your Bucket: Positive Strategies for Work and Life* offer seven questions that can help jump-start the relationship. Ask your employees:

1. "By what name do you like to be called?"
2. "What are your 'hot buttons'—hobbies or interests that you like to talk about a lot?"
3. "What increases your positive emotions, or 'fills your bucket,' the most?"
4. "From whom do you most like to receive recognition or praise?"
5. "What recognition or praise do you like best? Do you like public, private, verbal or other forms of recognition?"
6. "What form of recognition motivates you most?"
7. "What is the greatest recognition you have ever received?"

FAST TAKE 11
CRISIS MANAGEMENT

No matter what you do, odds are that at some point something catastrophic will happen to your organization.

Ian I. Mitroff, a professor at U.S.C., offers these management lessons for surviving a disaster.

Have the right heart. As Mitroff puts it: "Crises exact tremendous emotional costs; as a result, crises demand exceptional emotional capabilities."

Think. Not only do you have to think quickly to solve the problem, but you also need to think creatively. You are looking to make your organization stronger than it has ever been, not just to restore the status quo. That means supplementing what has worked with what will improve your company.

Maintain the right social and political skills. You will need everyone under you to buy in to your version of the future.

Have the right technical skills. Yes, you have to manage well, but you also need to know what must be done to restore the confidence and morale of your employees.

Know what to keep. In helping to build the new, stronger organization, don't throw out what has come before. Build off what has worked in the past.

CHAPTER 14

Marketing

When you strip away all the buzzwords, convoluted concepts, and hype, marketing is really pretty simple:

1. You figure out whom you want to sell to.
2. You figure out how you are going to get those people to buy what you have.

Then why is marketing so darn hard?

#36

Nothing happens in business until the customer says yes.

There are a bunch of reasons, as the best leaders understand. But the biggest problem is that we all tend to forget that absolutely nothing matters until there is a sale. And the only person who has the ability to open their wallet to pay for that sale is the customer.

Invariably, when you trace the ultimate failure of any marketing campaign, it always comes down to that the customer wasn't being offered something that they wanted, needed, or valued. Any other reason for failure is just a variation on the theme.

Of course, companies compound the felony by not selling through the right channels, creating bad (read: boring, confusing, misleading) advertising, employing less-than-terrific salespeople, pricing the product incorrectly, not offering the highest quality, giving poor service, and the like. But in the end, the problem always comes down to an inability to satisfy the customer.

Executives who succeed understand that.

Creating a customer

"The purpose of a business is to create a customer."

—Peter Drucker, sage

The customers decide what is important

"Companies are no longer setting the agenda for what customers want. They're finding out where the agenda is being set and enhancing it. The customers decide what's important. Your job is to listen and respond."

—Avram Miler, technology consultant

The three rules of advertising

"What are the three rules of advertising? Repetition, repetition, repetition."

—Al Ries, chairman,
Ries & Ries Consulting

Marketing that does not suck

"You need to do everything possible to guarantee that every marketing dollar you spend:
   a. Is set in a strategic context—that is, you know why you are spending it (for example, advertising 'because we have to advertise' is not a strategic context)
   b. Is based on a plan constructed to make certain that every marketing tactic and tool reinforces every other you are using
   c. Brings back more than $1 in return.
   "If . . . your plan doesn't meet the above criteria . . . your marketing sucks."

—Mark Stevens, president, MSCO,
and author, *Your Marketing Sucks!*

How to succeed in advertising

"The first thing one must do to succeed in advertising is to have the attention of the reader. That means to be interesting. The next thing is to stick to the truth, and that means rectifying whatever's wrong in the merchant's business. If the truth isn't tellable, fix it so it is. That is about all there is to it."

—John E. Powers, nineteenth-century copywriter

#37

If the dogs won't eat the dog food,
it is bad dog food. Period. Similarly,
if customers won't buy your product
or service, you are not giving them
what they either want or need.
It's your fault, not theirs.

Fresh and relevant

"You can never betray the core values of the brand, but you can work to make those values fresh and relevant. If you can't speak to people today, then you become an old icon."

—Chris Lowe, president, Foodservices
and Hospitality, Coca-Cola

Selling

"Don't confuse selling with art."

—Jack Taylor, vice chairman, Jordan, McGrath

A good match

"Selling is really about proving that you're a good match for your customer and then backing up your claim with facts. You may be able to make a one-time sale because you care, or because you're persuasive, or because you're enthusiastic and persistent. But you can't build a long-term relationship that way."

—Marilyn Carlson Nelson, co-chair, president,
and CEO, Carlson Companies

Memorable service

"We think ahead of the customer. Waiting for customers to tell you what they need is like driving your car by looking in the rearview mirror.

"Our job is to invent something that customers haven't thought of before. We want their experience here to be so wonderful that they become dependent on us. Because if people are dependent on us . . . they'll feel that they have to stay with us in order to function."

—Ali Kasikci, general manager,
Peninsula Beverly Hills Hotel

#38

Every communication with a customer must answer the two questions that they always have (even if they don't always express them to you): "What do you have and why should I care?"

When advertising doesn't work

"When advertising does not work, the client usually wasn't clear on the strategy he wanted the agency to deliver."

—C. J. Fraleigh, executive director of marketing
and advertising, General Motors

Who's the moron?

"The consumer isn't a moron. She is your wife."

—David Ogilvy

L.L.'s Golden Rule

"Sell good merchandise at a reasonable profit, treat your customers like human beings, and they will always come back for more."

—Leon Leonwood (L. L.) Bean

What people want

"Nobody wants to buy what you sell. What they want are the business results they can achieve by utilizing what you sell to pursue their own goals and objectives."

—Bill Stinnett, author, *Think Like Your Customer*

The essence of selling

"The essence of selling is understanding your customer's needs and convincing him that you're the best one to meet them."

—Fred Bialek, co-founder,
National Semiconductor Corp.

Wow

"One way to deliver smart service is to stop doing dumb things. That's why we have a 'kill a stupid rule' program. If an employee identifies a rule that prevents you from wow-ing customers, we will pay you $50."

—John Manning, vice president, Commerce Bank

Who's the boss?

"We tend to forget who pays our salaries. It's the customer."

—Lars Nyberg, chairman, NCR Corp.

When they don't care

"The worst sound in our business is silence. That means they don't care."

—Vince McMahon,
World Wrestling Entertainment

Boring always fails

"Memo to marketers: Boring always fails. Winners are remarkable."

—Seth Godin, marketing consultant,
author, *Purple Cow*

#39

Our three rules of advertising: Don't insult us, tell the truth, and have a sense of humor. Violate these rules at your own peril.

Numbers can only tell you so much

"I am convinced you cannot build a product out of consumer research. There isn't any consumer research that is so precise. The science isn't there, number one. And number two, consumers don't care nearly as much about the product as you do. It is hard for them to articulate, and it is hard for that articulation to be translated back into something you can read. Any time you are building a product based only on numbers you are going to get into big trouble."

—Roger Enrico, vice chairman, PepsiCo

Sell satisfaction

"No matter what you sell, you've got to sell satisfaction. This approach helped us build a clientele that is second to none in customer loyalty."

—Stanley Marcus, Neiman Marcus

Differentiate

"The biggest challenge facing companies in the 21st century will be to differentiate themselves from everyone else—to create a passionate following among customers who have too many choices.

"How do you create that kind of following? For one thing, by treating customers well. Simple politeness has become a lost art."

—Andy and Kate Spade, co-founders,
Kate Spade

The acid test

"If more CEOs had to go out and sell their products day in and day out, they'd pay a lot more attention to what they were making. When you are out there selling, there's no place to hide. It's the acid test."

—Jim Koch, CEO, Boston Brewing Co.

CREATING A CUSTOMER-FOCUSED ORGANIZATION

How do you make sure that your organization is customer-focused?

Ken Blanchard, who first achieved fame as the co-author of *The One Minute Manager*, sketches out the overarching strategy to take in *Customer Mania! It's Never Too Late to Build a Customer-Focused Company*:

Decide to do it. If you put your focus on pleasing customers, profits naturally follow.

Give customers want they want as they interact with every part of your company.

Treat employees correctly. Abused employees won't provide good service; those who are rewarded for taking care of customers will.

Make service a leadership priority. This, of course, starts the circle all over again, because if senior managers aren't committed to having their firm provide superior service, it is not going to happen. If they are, the message will permeate the ranks.

CHAPTER 15

The Organization and Corporate Culture

T he financial and business media typically say things like, "XYZ Corp. reported earnings of $1.23 a share," "International Widget announced that it was moving into five new markets," or "Acme Mousetrap Inc. said it would be laying off 5,000 people at the end of the quarter."

#40

We get the kind of organization we deserve.

But the reality is that an organization doesn't do anything. The only reason it succeeds—or doesn't—is because of the people involved.

A semantic distinction? We don't think so.

The problem with saying that organizations do this or that is that it makes it sound as if the people who work at those organizations have no control over the situation, that some monolithic force controls what goes on when we go to work.

That simply isn't true. Organizations are made up of people, and it is the people who determine what goes on at work. We are the ones responsible for both how the work gets done and how the organization functions.

The best leaders have already taken responsibility for that.

An organization is . . .

"Organizations are entities that enable society to pursue accomplishments that can't be achieved by individuals acting alone."

—James L. Gibson, author, *Organizations: Behavior, Structure, Processes*

Let people think!

"The real problem is that people do what they're told."

—David Maister, author, *First Among Equals*

Being highly effective

"Being highly effective as individuals and organizations is no longer optional . . . it is the price of entry."

—Stephen R. Covey, author, *The 8th Habit: From Effectiveness to Greatness*

Faith in the value of human potential

"Most business practices repress our natural tendency to have fun and to socialize. The idea seems to be that in order to succeed, you have to suffer. But I believe that you do your best work when you are feeling enthusiastic about things. Our business is based on faith in the value of human potential."

—George Zimmer, founder, The Men's Wearhouse

Building a strong culture

"You want to build a strong culture? Hold every manager accountable for the culture that he or she builds."

—Marcus Buckingham and Curt Coffman,
authors, *First Break All the Rules*

Be flexible

"I spend my time focusing on organizational and strategic flexibility. That involves a lot of unsexy things, including serious thinking about organizational-design options so that you can get the most out of your people, so that you only have to build things once, so that you reuse things, so that you have absolutely rigorous processes, and so that you can execute and deliver well."

—Andrea Anania, chief investment officer, Cigna

Is diversity a priority?

"If you want to find talented women and people of color for your organization, you can. But you have to make it a priority. And the last time I checked, priorities take money."

—Joe Watson, CEO, Strategic Hire

Different

"No matter who you are, you're going to have to work with people who are different from you. You're going to have to sell to people who are different from you, and buy from people who are different from you, and manage people who are different from you. This is how we do business. If it's not your destination, you should get off the plane now."

—Ted Childs, vice president of global
workforce diversity, IBM

Getting sloppy

"When you're making money and good margins, you tend to get sloppy."

—David Neeleman, CEO, JetBlue

Muda

"*Muda*. It's the one word of Japanese you really must know. It sounds awful as it rolls off your tongue and it should, because *muda* means 'waste,' specifically any human activity which absorbs resources but creates no *value*: mistakes which require rectification, production of items no one wants so that inventories and remainder goods pile up, processing steps which aren't actually needed . . . goods and services which don't meet the needs of the customer . . .

"It's hard to dispute—from even the most casual observation of what goes on during the average work day in the average organization—that *muda* is everywhere."

—James P. Womack, author,
Lean Thinking

#41

If you have a senior vice president of administration, something is terribly wrong. You shouldn't need a bureaucracy to manage the bureaucracy. In fact, you shouldn't have a bureaucracy at all.

The most powerful force in business

"The most powerful force in business isn't greed, fear, or even the raw energy of unbridled competition. The most powerful force in business is love. It's what will help your company grow and become stronger. It's what will propel your career forward. It's what will give you a sense of meaning and satisfaction in your work, which will help you do your best work."

—Tim Sanders, chief solutions officer, Yahoo!,
and author, *Love Is the Killer App*

Silos

"The biggest surprise [to me] . . . has been the strength of organizational forces that reinforce silos. We all know silos are bad. But it is just so hard to eliminate them. It's more than a full-time job. People are usually so busy doing 'their job,' that there's often not enough time for our job, which is to energize the behavior of the entire organization. Getting people to do that is much more complex than I ever expected."

—Leonard A. Schlesinger, COO, Limited Brands

The lessons that workers learn

"Prisoners learn early that the way to survive on the inside is to keep a low profile and follow orders. Sadly, that's the lesson that workers in most businesses learn."

—John Borchert, general manager, The Array Corp./
Prison Blues Clothing Line

The fundamentals of business

"The long-running successful organizations don't follow the paths of the moment or the latest trends. Their success is rooted in plain old solid and sustained execution of the fundamentals of business."

—Allan Gilmour, vice chairman,
Ford Motor Company

Masochists and sadists

"Organizations encourage at least half of their people to be masochists and the other half to be sadists."

—Harriet Rubin, author,
The Princessa: Machiavelli for Women

Profitable growth

"If businesses have a primal urge, it is the need for profitable growth. That growth is the source of value creation to shareholders. It is the gravitational pull that attracts and retains the best people. No business that has failed to grow has ever been able to maintain excellence over time."

—Chris Zook, head of global strategy practice,
Bain and Co.

Why meetings are boring

"Meetings are boring because they lack drama. Or conflict. This is a shame because most meetings have plenty of potential for drama, which is essential for keeping human beings engaged. Unfortunately, rather than mining for that golden conflict, most leaders of meetings seem to be focused on avoiding tension and ending their meetings on time. And while these may seem like noble pursuits, they lie at the heart of bad meetings.

"To make meetings less boring, leaders must look for legitimate reasons to provoke and uncover relevant, constructive ideological conflict. By doing so, they'll keep people engaged, which leads to more passionate discussions, and ultimately, to better decisions."

—Patrick M. Lencioni, author, *Death by Meeting*

The language of business

"The language of business is not the language of the soul or the language of humanity. It's a language of indifference; it's a language of separation, of secrecy, of hierarchy."

—Dame Anita Roddick, founder, The Body Shop

Focusing outward

"You have to get the right organization in place. You can have a wonderful culture . . . but if you have an organization that by its very nature generates a lot of internal—as opposed to external—activity, if you find yourself writing a lot of letters to people in the company, there's something wrong. You ought to be focused outwardly."

—Don Fites, chairman and CEO, Caterpillar

Organizational learning

"If [an] organization can't develop mechanisms for taking [what it learned] in the field and using it to become more agile, they're going to die."

—Jamie Gorelick, 9/11 Commission member and partner,
Wilmer Cutler Pickering Hale and Dorr

Auditioning the right people

"We believe [in the principle] of really getting the right people on [the] team—not only at headquarters but also inside the stores. . . . For example, we don't interview our crew members; we audition them. It takes a certain level of energy, enthusiasm, and outgoing personality to [work here]. We bring in five, six, seven people at a time and audition them for jobs. And you quickly learn which ones do or do not have the personality, charisma, and can-do attitude."

—Doug Ducey, president and CEO,
Cold Stone Creamery

The right goal

"Sound strategy starts with having the right goal. And I argue that the only goal that can support a sound strategy is superior profitability. If you don't start with that goal and seek it pretty directly, you will quickly be led to actions that will undermine strategy. If your goal is anything but profitability—if it's to be big, or to grow fast, or to become a technology leader—you'll hit problems."

—Michael Porter, professor, Harvard Business School,
and author, *Competitive Strategy: Techniques for
Analyzing Industries and Competitors*

#42

Ultimately, everything is personal.

Has anything really changed?

"Years ago when change was slow, markets were concentrated in a handful of countries and stability was the rule rather than the exception, an organizational approach that emphasized top-down hierarchy, rules and regulation and authority in the hands of executives dominated.

"In the 1970s, everything in the environment such as government regulation, information technology, global competition, union strength and influence, and customer demands and needs changed and pressures in how organizations operate dramatically increased.

"Unfortunately [more than 30 years later] many organizations have failed to change or adapt to their turbulent environments."

—James L. Gibson, author, *Organizations: Behavior, Structure, Processes*

No wealth without ideas

"There is no way to create wealth without ideas. Most new ideas are created by newcomers. So anyone who thinks the world is safe for incumbents is dead wrong."

—Gary Hamel, chairman, Strategos, and author, *Leading the Revolution*

Constructively dissatisfied

"You want to be constructively dissatisfied. When you've been successful and done great things, the biggest challenge is complacency. You need to fight that. We always need to think we can do better, be better."

—Michael L. Eskew, chairman and
chief executive officer, UPS

FAST TAKE
HOW TO BUILD A BETTER ORGANIZATION

Invariably, when someone is talking about design they'll say, "And, of course, form should follow function," the idea being that the shape of anything should be a natural reflection of the goal at hand.

That may work in designing products, but it has its flaws when it comes to building an organization. Invariably, a company's structure comes about by cobbling together various departments, all of which think they are the most vital to the organization's success.

The result? Regardless of what the organization chart depicts, you rarely have a neat, efficient flow of information.

To change that:

Have a plan. Picture what your ideal organization would look like.

Get buy-in. Invariably, people who will be affected by the new structure will have ideas you haven't thought of. Listen and adopt the best ones.

No side deals. Once the new structure is in place, everybody adjusts. It is more than possible that the chief technology officer hates the CFO. But if that is who the CTO should report to, she does. There are no exceptions made to accommodate (difficult) personalities.

Give it a while before making changes. Unless you discover that there is a horrible glitch that keeps work from getting done, give the new organizational form six months to a year before making any changes. You'll be amazed how many gripes will disappear if you wait.

CHAPTER 16
Teamwork and Partnerships

Accomplishing anything in business more complicated than opening the mail requires teamwork.

But how do you build a team?

There are lots of theories. Some people are big believers in biology, specifically in Darwin's survival of the fittest. You put the absolute best (smartest, most accomplished) people together and point them toward a goal.

Others believe in chemistry, feeling that only people who truly like one another and who work well together can get anything done.

We will leave chemistry and biology to the scientists. Our own inclination turns to a process that resembles journalism to describe how the best teams are put together.

Reporters try to answer five questions in telling stories: who, what, where, when, and why. (The best ones also add one more factor, how, but that ruins the alliteration.)

153

The people who are best at forging partnerships also ask five questions, according to consultants Richard H. Axelrod, Emily M. Axelrod, Julie Beedon, and Robert W. Jacobs, who have created a simple, straightforward primer on team building (*You Don't Have to Do It Alone: How to Involve Others to Get Things Done*) that we love.

No matter what project you are contemplating, they argue, the team-building process should always begin by asking:

- What kind of involvement is needed?
- Who needs to be included?
- How can we get them to participate?
- How do we keep them involved (i.e., engaged, motivated, and contributing at a high level)?
- How can we finish the project successfully?

We think that covers the fundamentals. For example, in deciding whom to include, of course, you need people with the expertise required to complete the task. But you can't stop there.

As part of your team, you also need people who care (otherwise nothing happens), people who will be affected by what you are doing (since they have an investment in the outcome), and those who have the authority to get the work accomplished. And you want to make sure that different points of view are represented in order to have the best ideas surface.

#43

> ## The whole *is* greater than the sum of its parts. If not, you have a serious management challenge on your hands.

It seems almost mandatory in talking about teamwork to draw a sports analogy. But the most common cliché happens to be one that is completely wrong. "There is no 'I' in team" is true only if you are talking about spelling bees. Teams, by definition, are made up of individuals, and all individuals have ego. Ignore that fact at your peril.

Let us point you to an acronym, one that probably can be found hanging in every high school locker room, but which is right on target, according to the leaders we talked with: T.E.A.M. = Together Everybody Achieves More.

When teams work well, that is exactly what happens.

Improvisation

"Improvisation is what cooking is all about. At the restaurant, we set the menu based on what's available that day. Food is alive, and it's changing all the time.

"Improvisation is also the key ingredient to collaboration. If you can work together and master the art of improvisation, there's no such thing as too many cooks in the kitchen."

—Alice Waters, founder, owner, and executive chef,
Chez Panisse

The four things that characterize great teams

"Four things characterize a great team. One, the team members must be galvanized by a common goal. That's what spurs people on and drives them to excel.

"Two, the members need to be driven by the team's results, not by individual results. For that to happen, you have to deal with the whole compensation issue. People must be able to subordinate their own goals—realistically—in favor of team goals.

"Three, the team has to be diverse. The team should be made up of people who think differently too—intuitive thinkers as well as logical thinkers. John F. Kennedy's cabinet comes to mind as a great example of a team made up of diverse thinkers.

"Four, on the best teams, no one hesitates to act out of a fear that what they're about to do isn't in their area of responsibility. Good team players take action. They don't stew about whether it's their job or about whether they're going to offend someone."

—Mike Maerz, co-founder, chairman,
and CEO, etrieve Inc.

Consensus

"I need to build consensus. I have 10 strong, passionate people on the leadership team who all have opinions. We have a long-term strategy, but we see it only as the outline of a puzzle. Every day, we have to react quickly to what is happening in the marketplace. I depend on the team to help me move the pieces of the puzzle every day."

—Mitchell Caplan, chief executive officer,
e-Trade

You need more diversity than you can imagine

"You need more diversity than you could imagine. I'm not talking about just gender or race. I mean diversity of skills and temperament. It's hard to get your team composition right. At the beginning, you need more diversity than you can imagine. When we started iVillage, we didn't have enough technical people or really anal analytical people. Instead, we had a surplus of people who could sell our story to customers and advertisers—which is great. But you still need people to build the subways. That lack of diversity slowed us down in the beginning.

"But as critical as diversity is at the beginning, once you start to scale, you want the opposite: a team of minds that think alike. Otherwise, you get gridlock."

—Candice Carpenter, co-founder,
iVillage Inc.

Every person is very important

"I learned that every person on our team is very important. If we don't have great dishwashers, then we can't serve you your meal—and then having the best food, the lowest prices, and the friendliest staff means nothing."

—Lloyd Hill, president and CEO, Applebee's

The best in people

"Today, it's employment at will. Nobody's here who doesn't want to be here. So, it's critical to understand people, to always be fair, and to want the best in them. And when it doesn't work, they need to know it's not personal."

—Jeffrey Immelt, chairman and CEO, General Electric

Is it a team or organizational politics?

"I view teams skeptically, because so many organizations treat them cynically. Teamwork has become a euphemism for organizational politics. Guess what? People sense the dishonesty there. People aren't stupid. They know when they're being used."

—Michael Schrage, co-director,
MIT Media Labs

#44

In well-run companies, everyone is needed but no one is indispensable. In other words, teamwork is built in.

Acting developmentally

"Imagine a manager who feels that she is at a dead end in her career. . . . What kind of career discussion would this person have with her direct reports? . . .

"A good solution for making an organization more developmental is to make sure that managers and leaders feel they have a clear career plan and developmental opportunities in their future. Leaders will act developmentally if they are being developed."

—John H. Zenger, author, *The Extraordinary Leader*

You can't do it alone

"Even the Lone Ranger didn't do it alone."

—Harvey MacKay, entrepreneur and author

Servant Leadership

"The idea is for the team leader to be at the service of the group. It should be clear that the team members own the outcome. The leader is there to bring intellectual, emotional, and spiritual resources to the team. Through his or her actions, the leader should be able to show the others how to think about the work that they're doing in the context of their lives. It's a tall order, but the best teams have such leaders."

—Franklin Jonath, president, Jonath & DiMeo Inc.

Check your ego at the door

"We think we're smarter than we are. The brightest individual doesn't necessarily make the best decision. The smarter decision usually comes from a team of people working together whose members recognize what they know and what they don't know.

"Teams work better when individual members check their egos at the door. I'm not proposing that we should be automatons, but if we all had a little less ego, the overall system would work much better than it does."

—Bo Peabody, chairman, Village Ventures

The two-pizza rule

"If you can't feed a team with two pizzas, the size of the team is too large."

—Jeff Bezos, chairman, CEO, and founder, Amazon.com

Being at ease

"A team works better when people are at ease with the leader."

—Michael Leinbach, shuttle launch director, NASA

A successful team?

"A successful team boils down to two things: mutual respect among team members and a common vision about where the team is going."

—Thomas C. Leppert, chairman and CEO, Turner Corp.

#45

Just because everyone wears the same uniform does not mean they are a team.

Working together

"One person working alone has to be really, really smart to solve such problems, and most people aren't that smart. It takes people working together to arrive at solutions."

—Jim Long, director of research, Herman Miller

The whole *is* greater

"None of us is as smart as all of us."

—Ken Blanchard, author, *The One Minute Manager*

Leading up

"As technology evolves and organizations decentralize, people on the front lines have more independence and responsibility. They are closer to the market and closer to how their product is used. They can see what their leaders are missing. When leaders falter, it's up to the rest of us to step up and help them lead. But leading up is not some noble calling: When you help those above you avoid a bad deal or seize an opportunity, you improve your whole organization's performance."

—Michael Useem, professor, Wharton School,
University of Pennsylvania

Partnering

"In today's complex world, operating without partners is not really an option for any but the simplest business. The real choice is whether you will partner deliberately or inadvertently, effectively or ineffectively, thoughtfully or carelessly."

—Jonathan Tisch, chairman and CEO, Loews Hotels

Human capital

"The most important form of capital is human capital; people are beginning to see themselves as assets. The social rules governing wealth that worked . . . are creaking."

—Stan Davis and Christopher Meyer, authors, *Blur*

Goals

"A team without goals is just another ineffective committee."

—James B. Miller, entrepreneur and author,
The Corporate Coach

FAST TAKE

LESSONS FROM THE HARDWOOD: YOU CAN'T FAKE IT

University of North Carolina basketball coach Dean Smith doesn't hold himself out as a business expert. But clearly his performance (he won more than three-quarters of the games he coached, including two national championships), establishes the Hall of Famer as someone who knows how to lead a team.

What does it take to lead successfully? Smith has a straightforward formula. Focus on factors within your control, and then make sure your people:

Play hard. You need to demand consistent effort.

Play together. Make sure everyone concentrates on team goals.

Play smart. Execute.

In other words, if you concentrate on the process—how your team performs—the results will take care of themselves.

FAST TAKE II
PROJECT MANAGEMENT 101

We all know how to get a project done on time.

However, on those occasions when things are not going as smoothly as you like, it may help to review these guidelines suggested by consultant Barry Flicker.

Avoid confusion through inclusion. This is an awkward phrase for an important point: Not only must everyone be clear on the objective, but there also needs to be communication between corporate layers to ensure that everyone understands the big picture as well as their individual tasks.

Shift from racing to pacing. In the rush to get things done yesterday, vital people can be left out of the loop, information can be overlooked, and mistakes can be made. The moral: Slow from a mad dash to a swift canter.

Both the project and the people must be fulfilled. Employees who don't feel a personal commitment to the task at hand do the minimum.

Work from "the zone." Eliminating stress allows people to do their best work. To help eliminate that stress, help come up with a solution, instead of merely complaining about being overworked.

Every manager worth his reserved parking space knows all this, of course. (Smart employees do, too.) But, as the missed deadlines, frustration, and finger-pointing that can accompany a major project show, there is a huge chasm between knowing what to do and doing it.

CHAPTER 17
Risk

When thinking about risk, the first thing many of us recall is the truism from investing: No risk, no reward.

**Let us edit a long-standing cliché:
No *prudent* risk, no *fairly predictable* rewards.**

That adage, absolutely true when it comes to where we put our money, has far broader applications.

There is risk in every human endeavor. That's why in the pages ahead you are going to read the words of leaders who seem to spend an inordinate amount of time trying to figure out what could go wrong. They are trying to reduce risk.

For many, the word risk conjures images of riverboat gamblers, wildcatters, and the proverbial million-to-one shot. While taking wild chances certainly happens, that isn't what we will be talking about in the pages ahead. We will be discussing a concept that at first sounds like an oxymoron: prudent risk. But that's how the best businesspeople approach an uncertain situation: They analyze the situation, consider what could go wrong, and chart a well-reasoned course.

Every decision involves risk. If you don't take risks—not stupid risks, but calculated ones—you are never going to be able to accomplish anything.

The kind of risks you take define you as a leader.

Paranoia

"I believe in the value of paranoia. Business success contains the seeds of its own destruction. The more successful you are, the more people want a chunk of your business and then another chunk and then another until there is nothing left. I believe that the prime responsibility of a manager is to guard constantly against other people's attacks and to inculcate this guardian attitude in the people under his or her management."

—Andy Grove, chairman, Intel

Set an example

"If you want risk taking, set an example yourself and reward and praise those that do."

—Jack Welch, former chairman
and CEO, GE

Confront reality to minimize risk

"It appears to me more appropriate to follow up the real truth of a matter than the imagination of it; for many have pictured republics and principalities which in fact have never been known or seen, because how one lives is so far distant from how one ought to live, that he who neglects what is done for what ought to be done, sooner effects his ruin than his preservation; for a man who wishes to act entirely up to his professions of virtue soon meets with what destroys him among so much that is evil."

—Niccolò Machiavelli

The fates, the gods, or ourselves

"Why, given their advanced mathematical ideas, did the Arabs not proceed to probability theory and risk management? The answer, I believe, has to do with their view of life. Who determines our future: the fates, the gods, or ourselves? The idea of risk management emerges only when people believe that they are to some degree free agents."

—Peter Bernstein, author, *Against the Gods: The Remarkable Story of Risk*

The past isn't always prologue

"Managing risk means thinking about the future, not about the past....We all get comfortable basing our strategies for the future on the past. That's why risks that we didn't anticipate can take us by surprise—and why it's so hard to reckon with events for which there is no precedent."

—Ron Dembo, president and CEO, Algorithmics

Ten reasons we're going to go out of business

"I keep a list of the 10 most serious threats to the company. The lawyers hate this. It's actually called 'Ten reasons we're going to go out of business.' It definitely focuses the mind as much as the prospect of imminent hanging. So we ask ourselves, If we end up failing, what will be the reason? ... Working on the risk-factor section is my favorite part of drafting prospectuses. It lets you look at your company and say, Okay, what might go wrong?"

—Marc Andreessen, founder,
Netscape and Loudcloud

Test

"Test, test, test. A person with an idea and no data is another person with an opinion."

—John Chapin, co-founder, LifeMinders Inc.

Risk is not a four-letter word

"When did risk become a four-letter word? ...

"Even in a slow-growth economy, companies can't win big in the marketplace by doing things only a little bit better than the competition. Even in a conservative environment, it's hard to deliver a truly compelling message to customers if you sound like everyone else. Even with an unforgiving climate on Wall Street, merely cutting bottom-line costs doesn't do much to spur top-line growth."

Keith Hammonds, deputy editor,
Fast Company

No one person has the answer

"We want really smart people who have tremendous passion, great conviction and courage, and a little bit of willingness to go out there and take a risk, because when you're working in an industry that is evolving rapidly, no one person has the right answer for anything."

—Dan Rosensweig, COO, Yahoo!

Every decision involves risk

"People can spend months debating the 'best' decision without actually arriving at any decision. Every decision involves risk. And if there are 10 ways to do something, 8 of them will probably work. So pick 1 of the 8 and get going. Life's too short. You have more 10 decisions to make after this 1."

—David House, CEO, Bay Networks

Don't be so quick to start a business

"My advice to young entrepreneurs? Don't be so quick to run out and start a business. Young people today think they'll miss their big chance if they don't get involved in a startup immediately. But what many people don't recognize is that the basic skills of building a company are the same today as they were 20 years ago: Know how to create customers, deliver on your promises, and keep your costs lower than your revenue. The problem is that many people are simply too inexperienced to start their own business."

—Frank S. Greene, founding partner,
New Vista Capital

Risk at its core

"Risk at its core is about nothing less than survival."

—David Ropeik, author, *Risk*

Leave a big legacy

"The possibility of failure is like a vagrant ghost that wanders around with you and causes you to be anxious. But it's hard to do anything that will have some measure of impact unless you take risks. If you take the easy way, the comfortable way, or the safe way, you're not going to leave a big legacy."

—Jack Valenti, former head of the
Motion Picture Association of America

HOW TO BE A RISK TAKER

What separates the risk takers—be they people or organizations—from the rest of us?

After 10 years of studying these people, the following are our conclusions. Risk takers are:

Not overly preoccupied with making mistakes. All the old clichés—such as "Even the best hitters in baseball fail 7 out of 10 times"—hold true here. Successful risk takers learn from their mistakes but don't brood about them.

Willing to admit when they are wrong. They kill the project and start another.

Relentlessly upbeat. They minimize the downside and focus on what could go right.

CHAPTER 18

Social Responsibility, Trust, and Ethics

I f you want to understand why social responsibility, trust, and ethics are business issues, spend a few minutes with James E. Burke.

Burke, named one of the ten best managers of the twentieth century by *Fortune* magazine, had a stellar career at Procter & Gamble and later Johnson & Johnson (J&J), where during his 13-year tenure as chairman and CEO he steadily increased sales, earnings, and the company's share price.

But Burke is best remembered as the man who steered Johnson & Johnson through the Tylenol crisis. In the fall of 1982, seven people in Chicago died after taking Extra-Strength Tylenol capsules laced with cyanide. (Tylenol is made by a J&J subsidiary.)

Even though he was convinced that it was an act of sabotage—a fact later proven by authorities—Burke moved quickly to quell consumer panic. He pulled every Tylenol product off the shelf everywhere, even though Tylenol generated closed to $500 million in revenues for the company. The move cost J&J $130 million.

And then Burke did something the experts said was impossible. He reintroduced the brand six weeks later—with triple-sealed safety packaging, a first for any consumer product—convinced that consumers would hold neither the brand nor the company that made it responsible for the deaths. The move worked. Tylenol had 85 percent of its former market share back in a year, and by the end of year two, sales were greater than they had been before the murders.

**You can't be a little bit ethical.
Either you are ethical or you are not.
There is no in-between.**

To what does Burke attribute his successful career in general and the skillful handling of the Tylenol crisis (which is now a Harvard Business School case study) in particular?

"It's all about trust.

"Recently, I tried to figure out how I got so lucky in my business life, and I have been as lucky as anyone I know. The question was why.

"Coming up with the answer wasn't easy. Nothing immediately came to mind, so I started to write down all the people who had influenced me from the beginning. The list included my parents, of course, my friends, my teachers, and all of a sudden it became clear to me that everyone on the list had one thing in common. They had each beaten me over the head with the same idea: the importance of trust, of telling the truth, of keeping your word and doing what you said you were going to do.

"And so I did. I don't doubt that I am smart. I have certain intellectual gifts. But maybe the smartest thing I ever did was to become trustworthy."

It is a priceless asset to have in your career and—as you are about to see—throughout an organization.

You can't teach honesty

"If people are dishonest, a course won't make them honest."

—Tom Campbell, former dean, Haas School of Business,
University of California

Trust your associates

"If you don't trust your associates to know what is going on, they'll know you don't really consider them partners."

—Don Soderquist, vice chairman, Wal-Mart

Integrity transcends borders

"Integrity transcends borders, language and culture. It is not something that we can impose, but it is something we can influence and monitor."

—Rick Wagoner, chairman and CEO, General Motors

A good corporate citizen

"There has been a tendency in the business world to confuse citizenship with philanthropy. They're not the same thing. Enron was a great philanthropist, and clearly it was not a good corporate citizen. The heart of global citizenship is about ethics and conduct."

—Debra Dunn, senior vice president, Hewlett-Packard

Intent

"Business integrity means living up to the intent and not just the letter of the law."

—Fred Hassan, chairman and CEO,
Schering-Plough

For trust to take hold

"For trust to take hold, the first thing a leader must do is generate shared values, goals, visions or objectives with those she wishes to lead."

—Warren Bennis, professor, U.S.C.

The less we make, the less we have to give away

"This is a business, and businesses need profits to survive. The less we make, the less we will have to give away, and the less other companies will think we have a mission that is worth imitating."

—Yvon Chouinard, founder, Patagonia

No trust, no deal

"Reputation is the primary attribute of commercial relationships. If there is no trust, there's no deal, period."

—Kevin T. Jackson, professor, Fordham University

The avenues to express greed

"It is not that humans have become any more greedy than in generations past. It is that the avenues to express greed have grown so enormously."

—Alan Greenspan, chairman, Federal Reserve

Good business

"Just as good deeds in life create unforeseen blessings, I believe it is fundamental that honesty and integrity will ultimately create business success. Creating an ethical business culture should not be viewed as a sacrifice. Indeed, it is *good business* to be open and honest with your shareholders. It is *good business* to have fair dealings with your business partners. It is *good business* to reward employees for being honest and ethical. It is *good business* to be known as a company that deals fairly in its business transactions. It is *good business* for shareholders to know that a company not only has a code of ethics but that the code is followed every day. It is also *good business* to select CEOs and Presidents largely based on their integrity and commitment to ethical behavior."

—Roel C. Campos, commissioner,
U.S. Securities and Exchange Commission

Be completely forthright

"Having integrity means more to us than simply the absence of deception. It means we are completely forthright in all our dealings. We say what needs to be said, not simply what people want to hear."

—Scott Cook, founder and chairman of
the executive committee, Intuit

Two-way communication

"Open, honest, two-way communication is the bedrock of ethical standards."

—Edward M. Liddy, chairman and CEO,
Allstate

#48

Everybody must understand *and*
internalize the company's core values.
Doing so frees up time, because you
don't have to debate the organization's
core beliefs. Everyone knows what they
are. It also frees resources. When
people know what they are supposed
to do, they need less supervision.

Trust your employees

"At some level, you have to trust your employees are doing the right things."

—Sandy Hughes, head of Procter & Gamble's global privacy council, in explaining why the company does not do extensive monitoring of employee activities

The power of truth

"In the post-Enron, post-WorldCom era, much has been written on corporate governance, corporate responsibility, financial malfeasance, and greed. The perp walks of business executives have become a regular feature of the nightly news. . . .

"However, in the wake of those scandals, we've changed: We've rediscovered the power of truth. We'll no longer be willing to be patient with people who claim that they weren't really lying but were simply shading the truth. . . .

"Truth will be the mantra of business. . . . We, as consumers, investors, and members of society, will demand it."

—Patrick T. Harker, dean, Wharton School, University of Pennsylvania

Courage!

"I believe we're all born with courage deep inside us. It may be latent for decades, but it's always there, waiting for us to find it."

—Bill George, former chairman and CEO, Medtronics

The worst crime

"I want to tell you socialists that I have studied your philosophy—I have heard your orators—I have kept close watch upon your doctrines for 30 years and know how you think and what you propose. I know too what you have up your sleeve. Economically you are unsound; socially you are wrong; industrially you are an impossibility. . . . The worst crime against working people is a company that fails to make a profit."

—Samuel Gompers, founder,
American Federation of Labor

Intimacy

"Trust, which is the glue of business, is created by dependability, quality content, and intimacy with clients. Of those elements, intimacy is the hardest to achieve. If you ever listen to Frank Sinatra sing, it sounds as if he's singing directly to you. That was Sinatra's great skill, and that's what we try to achieve in our business. We want to connect with people on a human level—to touch them in some way."

—George Forrester Colony, chairman and CEO,
Forrester Research Inc.

How would my actions appear?

"For a long time we wrestled with how to describe an appropriate standard of behavior for our employees. Finally, we got it right. We tell our people that they should always ask themselves: 'How would my actions appear if they were described tomorrow on the front page of the local paper?' When you ask the question that way, things get real clear."

—Carl Sewell, the most successful luxury car dealer
in the United States

Worse than having no policy at all

"It is not enough for reporting companies simply to have a code of ethics. No matter how well or beautifully the language of the code of ethics reads, if the code is relegated to the back of a policy manual or a cluttered website, it is of no use. I submit that having a code of ethics that is not vigorously implemented is worse than not having a code of ethics. It smacks of hypocrisy."

—Roel C. Campos, commissioner,
U.S. Securities and Exchange Commission

#49

If it is not right, don't do it; if it is not true, don't say it.

Growing a substantial economy

"Are the needs of the corporation and world in conflict? In the long run, they can't be. Today, 600 million of the Earth's inhabitants enjoy the material benefits of industrialism. Some 2.5 billion more—China, India and the former Soviet republics—will join us. The final 3 billion people will follow. To accommodate all those people in terms of resources today, we would need three planets. So how can the needs of the world be met in the future? The truth is we can't build a sustainable economy. We can only grow one. That's a lesson I learned from the rain forest. The vitality of nature comes from its capacity to cultivate more advanced forms of life and then support them for billions of years on finite resources and a fixed flow of energy from the sun."

—Tachi Kiuchi, managing director, Mitsubishi Electric Corp.

An economic incentive

"Businesses can talk about all of this social responsibility stuff, but they are likely to do something about it only if there's an economic reason for them to do it.

"Consider the companies that voluntarily reduced their greenhouse gas emissions. They recognized that ... processes that use less carbon are generally better economically because they're more fuel efficient.

"But to expect companies simply to be socially responsible without an economic incentive is asking a lot."

—Bill Joy, founder and former chief scientist,
Sun Microsystems

FAST TAKE

WHY SOCIAL RESPONSIBILITY, TRUST, AND ETHICS ARE BUSINESS ISSUES

Behaving well—telling the truth, keeping your word, and performing in an exemplary manner—is a form of competitive advantage.

If you look at the companies (and businesspeople) who have been successful over time, behaving well is a hallmark of each and every one of them. Yes, crooks can make a lot of money in the short run. But over the long term, the companies that are successful—Johnson & Johnson, Procter & Gamble, Target—are trustworthy. It is hard to find a successful company that isn't. Similarly, you'd be hard pressed to find a businessperson with a similar record of success who has not been trustworthy as well.

In other words, trust is a business strategy.

It used to be that we all expected companies and businesspeople to keep their word, do what they said they would do, and put out a good product or service.

That used to be the price of entry. It no longer is.

Because being trustworthy is no longer a given, you (and your company) have an advantage if you are. Today, being trustworthy is a business asset. It helps your company if you make a mistake, because people are more forgiving of companies that have earned their trust, and it gives you some pricing power.

Prove it, you say? It's easy. Simply test what people are

willing to pay for your product with your name on it, versus the identical product without the name attached. If there is a premium, you are trustworthy. Trust is real, palpable, and bankable.

CHAPTER 19

Speed

There is probably no better example of the power of speed than what happens in the pits at an Indy car race.

Here's what the pit crews say is important if you are going to move quickly:

1. **The faster you go, the more you need to talk**. Everyone needs to be clear about what is going to be done by whom and when. Constant communication is vital.
2. **Don't panic when someone overtakes you early on.** Stick with what got you here.
3. **Whatever it takes, stay in the race.** Keep moving and fix problems on the fly whenever possible.
4. **Make the most of downtime.** It is inevitable that there will be some downtime. Make the necessary repairs and reenergize.

Why our interest in pit crews and speed? It's simple. Your organization needs to move faster than ever before.

#50

In today's economy, it's the fast companies that trounce the slow.

Competition these days can come from anywhere—from down the street, from across the ocean, or through the Web. If you have any hope of staying in business, you have to stay ahead of them. And that, as the best leaders know, requires speed, moving quickly to do the right things. Among other things, that means reducing your cycle time, increasing how fast you respond to competitive threats, and getting your product to market.

Counterintuitive as it may seem, your effort to move faster may need to begin with a step back.

Experts say your first move should be to systematically eliminate everything that is keeping your organization from moving faster now. What are the roadblocks? Where are the bottlenecks? Eliminate them and things will get done faster, even without a directive from the top.

In other words, streamlining the organization should be your first objective.

Faster

"If you want to run a world-class company today, you have to track far more and do it far faster."

—William H. Gates III, chairman, Microsoft

Do the things that will allow you to be fast

"Success is not just about being fast. It's about doing all of the things that allow you to be fast."

—J. Neil Weintraut, general partner,
21st Century Venture Partners

Fast teams need clear goals

"Team members need ultraclear priorities in order to work fast. You need to say, 'Our goal is to sell $2 billion a month on the Web,' and then work with our team to achieve that goal."

—Steve Ward, chief information officer and
vice president of business transformation, IBM

The acceleration trap

"Essential as positive energy is for driving corporate performance, unless one manages that energy with insight and wisdom, it can degenerate into severe pathologies. The greatest danger? Falling into the acceleration trap. Seeing what companies can accomplish during phases of intensive energy, some CEOs assume that the exceptional can become the routine. Following the Olympic motto 'always more, always faster, always higher,' they drive their organizations constantly at and beyond the edge of their capabilities. This effort to achieve a state of permanent acceleration ultimately leads to organizational burnout. The company and its people simply become exhausted."

—Heike Bruch and Sumantra Ghoshal,
authors, *A Bias for Action*

Do it right

"If you do it first and you do it right, you can win pretty big. But it's much better to do it right than first."

—Kevin O'Connor, founder, DoubleClick,
and author, *The Map of Innovation*

First off the mark wins

"Can you take a product and get it to market faster than anyone else? That is what the game is about every time."

—Ray Blair, director of e-procurement, IBM

#51

Look to streamline your operation everywhere. The cumulative effect can be astonishing.

Catalyst

"As with all catalysts, the manager's function is to speed up the reaction between two substances, thus creating the desired end product. Specifically, the manager creates performance in each employee by speeding up the reaction between the employee's talents and the company's goals."

—Marcus Buckingham and Curt Coffman, authors,
First Break All the Rules

What everyone in the organization must know

"Unless *everyone* in the organization knows the guiding principles, practices them, and is seen practicing them, they are a waste of time and ultimately a demoralizer. They will slow you down, not speed you up."

—Jason Jennings and Laurence Haughton, authors,
It's Not the Big That Eat the Small . . .
It's the Fast That Eat the Slow

#52

Just because you occasionally step on the accelerator doesn't mean you can keep it floored indefinitely. Organizations can run flat out only for short periods.

Over-satisfying your customers

"In their efforts to stay ahead by developing competitively superior products, many companies don't realize the speed at which they are moving up-market, over-satisfying the needs of their original customers, as they race the competition toward higher-performance, higher-margin markets. In doing so, they create a vacuum at lower price points into which competitors employing disruptive technology can enter."

—Clayton M. Christensen, professor,
Harvard Business School, and author,
The Innovator's Solution

First mover advantage

"If there is one thing that has become apparent in the short history of the on-line economy it is the Holy Grail of first mover advantage is as elusive as it is exaggerated."

—Sydney Finkelstein, professor,
Tuck School of Business, Dartmouth College

Speed kills

"Speed wins [but] speed [also] kills—brands and products just don't have the time to develop the old way."

—Seth Godin, author,
Unleashing the Idea Virus

Some things should not be accelerated

"The problem is that our love of speed, our obsession with doing more and more in less and less time, has gone too far; it has turned into an addiction, a kind of idolatry. Even when speed starts to backfire, we invoke the go-faster gospel. Falling behind at work? Get a quicker Internet connection. . . . Diet not working? Try liposuction. . . . And yet some things cannot, should not, be sped up. They take time; they need slowness. When you accelerate things that should not be accelerated, when you forget how to slow down, there is a price to pay."

—Carl Honoré, author,
In Praise of Slowness

FAST TAKE
HOW TO BE FAST

Managers at Dell will tell you that speed is the ultimate competitive weapon. (Analysts and the competition agree that it is the key to the computer company's success.)

Here is Dell's five-point plan for building a really fast company—and their plan works even if you don't sell direct.

The supply chain starts with the customer. By cutting out retailers and selling directly to customers, Dell is in a far better position to forecast real consumer demand. If you have to use middlemen, as retailers such as Wal-Mart do, you can obtain this sort of information by monitoring every sale in real time

Replace inventory with information. To operate with close to zero inventory, Dell communicates constantly with its suppliers—several times a day.

If you can't measure it, you can't manage it. Dell knows what works because it measures everything—inventory, cash, time to build a computer. Once they have the numbers, they concentrate on improving them.

Complexity slows you down. Dell cut the number of its core suppliers from several hundred to about 25 and standardized everything it could.

Work to become radically faster. Dell sets out to obtain massive improvement, not incremental change. For example, the goal is not 3 percent faster production, but 30 percent.

CHAPTER 20
Strategy and Growth

n the movie *Annie Hall*, Alvy Singer (played by Woody Allen) tells Annie Hall (Diane Keaton) that their relationship is in trouble. "A relationship is like a shark," says Alvy. "It has to constantly keep moving forward or it dies."

It's the same with companies. Either they grow or they die. No matter what strategy a company decides to pursue—growing from within or through acquisition, becoming the low-cost producer in the market or dominating the high end of the market by acquiring every other firm in that niche—it must produce increased revenues.

Former MIT professor Michael Treacy, co-author of *The Discipline of Market Leaders*, suggests five strategies that managers can follow to increase revenues. Our experience argues that at least one of them should be an integral part of whatever strategy your company ultimately decides to pursue.

#53

If you don't know where you are going,
any road will take you there. You need
a clear strategy and a clear direction,
one that everyone in the organization
understands as well as you do.

1. **If you want to grow, you can't afford to shrink.** Concentrate first on retaining the customers you already have. Every one you lose means one you have to gain just to stay even. And it is far more expensive to acquire new customers than to hold on to the ones you already have.

2. **Look for areas where growth is likely to happen.** Parse market data in every conceivable way to spot the next big trend. Then target your resources to get there before the competition does.

3. **Invade adjacent markets.** Extend what you do. If you are selling routers, think about providing cable, software, computers, and service contracts.

4. **Develop a related line of business.** Think about what makes sense given what you already do best. If you are a fast-food hamburger chain, why not start a string of restaurants that concentrates on selling chicken?

5. **Take business from your competitors.** This is, of course, the most difficult of the five options. You need to develop a competitive advantage to distinguish your product or service from your competitors'. It doesn't matter what strategy, or strategies, you choose. What

matters is that you have one—and, as we saw in Chapter 7, that you execute it.

Winning with ideas

"Organizations today must not only outgun and outhustle competitors, they must also outthink them. Companies win with ideas. Just consider the differing fates of Westinghouse and General Electric.

"Westinghouse certainly had a culture of product innovation: Commercial radio, commercial nuclear power, air brakes, and lots of other amazing inventions came out of Westinghouse. But its managerial culture was incredibly insular. . . . Innovation, such as it was, was devoted to thinking, 'Should we keep this business or sell it off?' For all its product breakthroughs, Westinghouse is a dead organization—its businesses have been dismantled and sold.

"By contrast, GE—even before Jack Welch—has been an idea (and profit) machine. It's a prime example of a company that embraces a few big ideas—boundarylessness, Six Sigma, service businesses, digitization—and executes them really well. Once an idea becomes a corporate initiative, it gets embedded into the company's way of managing itself. These key initiatives are discussed and monitored in at least one management meeting every month. GE doesn't just talk about ideas, it gives them a bear hug, and we all know the result: GE sits at the top of the industrial heap."

—Thomas H. Davenport, professor of information technology and management, Babson College

Do it!

"Just do it—and worry about it later."

—Jimmy Pedro, marketing vice president, Monster.com

How can you be put out of business?

"Always ask yourself how someone could preempt your product or service. How can they put you out of business? Is it price? Is it service? Is it ease of use? No product is perfect and if there are good competitors in your market, they will figure out how to abuse you."

—Mark Cuban, co-founder, Broadcast.com,
and owner, Dallas Mavericks

Greed *is* good

"I have never known much good done by those who affected to trade for the public good. It is an affectation, indeed, not very common among merchants, and very few words need be employed in dissuading them from it."

—Adam Smith, eighteenth-century economist,
author, *The Wealth of Nations*

The basics of commerce

"The basics of commerce don't change: You've got to have something that people need, something that they can't get elsewhere. And the more they can't get it elsewhere, the more they need it."

—Michael Bloomberg, founder, Bloomberg LP,
and mayor of New York City

A good strategic plan

"The more clear and concise your strategic plan is, the easier it is to implement and the less that can go wrong along the way."

—William A. Cohen, strategy consultant

Authorship

"I think it is very difficult to lead today when people are not really participating in the decision. You won't be able to attract and retain great people if they don't feel they are part of the authorship of the strategy and the authorship of really crucial issues. If you don't give people an opportunity to be engaged, they won't stay."

—Howard Schultz, founder, Starbucks

Keep moving

"Like competition itself, competitive advantage is a constantly moving target. For any company in any industry, the key is not to get stuck with a single simple notion of its source of advantage. The best competitors, the most successful ones, know how to keep moving and always stay on the cutting edge."

—George Stalk, Jr., senior vice president,
Boston Consulting Group

Shoot first

"Somewhere out there is a bullet with your company's name on it . . . a competitor that will render your strategy obsolete. You've got to shoot first."

—Kenneth Lay, perhaps anticipating Enron's demise

Timing

"The time to go into a new business is when it's badly run by others."

—Sir Richard Branson, founder, Virgin

Audaciousness

"Ultimately, what separates a winner from a loser at the grand master level is the willingness to do the unthinkable. A brilliant strategy is, certainly, a matter of intelligence, but intelligence without audaciousness is not enough.

"So it is in business. One does not succeed by sticking to convention. When your opponent can easily anticipate every move you make, your strategy deteriorates."

—Garry Kasparov, former number-one-ranked chess player

#54

As IBM's Tom Watson would say: Think!

Visionaries

"There's a very small percentage of CEOs who are visionary, who have the courage to follow their own assessment of a market that's developing . . . that nobody says is there."

—John Thompson, vice chairman, Heidrick & Struggles

Outrageous goals

"No person or firm will ever achieve greatness without an outrageous objective."

—Bill Davidson, founder, MESA Research

Win, place, or don't show

"The winners . . . will be those who search out and partic-ipate in the real growth industries and insist on being num-ber one or number two in every business they're in—the number one or number two leanest, lowest-cost worldwide producers of quality goods and services or those who have a clear technological edge, a clear advantage in the market niche.

"Where we are not number one or number two and don't have, or can't see, a route to a technological edge we've got to ask ourselves Peter Drucker's very tough question: If you weren't already in this business, would you enter it today?

"And if the answer is no, face that second difficult ques-tion: What are you going to do about it?"

—Jack Welch, former CEO of GE,
and author, *Winning*

Change from the top

"Most leadership strategies are doomed to failure from the outset. As people have been noting for years, the majority of strategic initiatives that are driven from the top are mar-ginally effective—at best. Corporate reorganizations are even more common than new strategies, but how many reorganizations actually produce companies that are dra-matically more effective than they were before? Throw in mergers and acquisitions: Look at all of those that have failed. The traditional model of change—change that is led from the top—has a less-than-impressive track record."

—Peter Senge, author, *The Fifth Discipline*

Don't be a prisoner of your business model

"There are two contradictory axioms in business. One says that when you figure out what makes you successful, take the cookie-cutter approach: Don't change a thing and be the best at that. The other says that you have to continue evolving in order to take advantage of new opportunities. I chose the latter. I didn't want to be a prisoner of our business model."

—David Neeleman, founder and CEO, JetBlue

What strategy is

"Executives . . . say, 'We have a strategy.' But typically, their 'strategy' is to produce the highest-quality products at the lowest cost or to consolidate their industry. They're just trying to improve on best practices. That's not a strategy. . . .

"There's a fundamental distinction between strategy and operational effectiveness. Strategy is about making choices, trade-offs; it's about deliberately choosing to be different. Operational effectiveness is about things that you really shouldn't have to make choices on; it's about what's good for everybody and about what every business should be doing."

—Michael Porter, professor,
Harvard Business School

You don't have to be first

"The individuals or companies who create radically new markets are not necessarily the ones to scale them up into mass markets. Indeed, the evidence shows that in the majority of the cases, they almost never [do]."

—Constantinos C. Markides and Paul A. Geroski,
authors, *Fast Second: How Smart Companies Bypass
Radical Innovation to Enter and Dominate New Markets*

Why we handle difficult problems so badly

"When you are in a tough position—such as dealing in anticipation of your business being hurt—you tend to think very conventionally, because you don't really want to deal with it. What you tend to do is say, 'This is no big deal. It will never work.'"

—-Roger Enrico, vice chairman, PepsiCo

Overcome obstacles

"When we left the Los Angeles airport we were headed for Dallas, but within 20 minutes the situation had changed. The wind currents were a little different than predicted, so we were slightly off course. The captain made a minute adjustment and we were again headed for Dallas. He didn't turn the plane around and return to L.A. to make a fresh start. As you head toward your goals, be prepared to make some slight adjustments in your course. You don't change your decision to go—you do change your direction to get there."

—Zig Ziglar, author, *See You at the Top*

Stay loose

"Plan carefully. Figure out as much as you can beforehand: suppliers and distributors to use, customers to target, people to hire. But don't be afraid to explore other paths if only some—or none—of your initial plan works out. And don't be afraid to admit that you've made a mistake."

—Barrett Hazeltine, professor,
Brown University

Warriors don't make good CEOs

"The kinds of companies we admire today are also those that depend increasingly on female attributes. We are in the relationship era: It's all about getting close to customers, striking up joint ventures, partnering with suppliers. Warriors don't make good CEOs in companies based on relationships."

—Janice Gjertsen, CEO, Coaching Circles

FAST TAKE
A MANAGER'S STRATEGY PRIORITY LIST

Picture what the successful company of tomorrow will look like. It might make it easier to figure out what you should be doing today. That was the premise *The Economist*'s management editor, Frances Cairncross, took in listing the top 10 things companies will need to do to be successful in the years ahead.

1. *Manage knowledge.* "A company is the sum of what its people understand and do well."
2. *Make decisions.* "Good judgment will remain a key skill."
3. *Focus on customers.*
4. *Manage talent.*
5. *Manage collaboration.*
6. *Build the right structure.* "As costs of handling information decline, new opportunities open for redefining the corporate shape."
7. *Manage communications.*
8. *Set standards.* "Ironically, Internet technologies, tools of freedom and decentralization, call for discipline, protocols and standard processes."
9. *Foster openness.*
10. *Develop leadership.* "Without the right organizational structure, culture and staff, a company will not fully benefit from even the most sophisticated technology."

CHAPTER 21
The Link Between Success and Failure

F. Scott Fitzgerald once said there are no second acts in American life. That is a pithy statement. It is profound.

And it is also completely wrong.

The United States in general and the business world in particular are home to many successful second acts.

The people who founded America came here looking to begin a second act in their lives, extremely unhappy about how the first act had gone. They set a precedent that continues to this day.

#55

If you haven't had one spectacular failure in your life, you haven't tried hard enough.

The success that so many leaders achieve is often the direct result of a second act. Why? Because so many of them failed in the first act. Business leaders will talk endlessly about how their failure was a formative experience—and how without it they never would have learned how to be successful.

The moral? If at first you don't succeed . . .

Tough times build character

"Tough times build character. The best thing that ever happened to me was when the Great Depression hit, and my father couldn't give me one more dollar for college. In order to return to school, I had to learn to be self-reliant, resourceful, and diligent. . . . When dealt a bad hand, you learn to play smarter."

—Sir John Marks Templeton,
mutual fund founder

Boring your way to success

"The next time somebody accuses you of being plain vanilla, bore them to death with success."

—Harvey MacKay, author, *Swim with the Sharks*

Becoming stronger

"Failure is just part of the culture of innovation. Accept it and become stronger."

—Albert Yu, senior vice president and
strategic program director, Intel

What we do wrong

"It's a misnomer that our talents make us a success. They help, but it's not what we do well that enables us to achieve in the long run. It's what we do wrong and how we correct it that ensures our long lasting success."

—Bernie Marcus, co-founder, Home Depot

Feel sorry for yourself?

"My God, you are going to feel sorry for yourself? George Washington slept in a tent for seven years!"

—James Dimon, president and COO,
JPMorgan Chase

Failure

"There are no easy businesses. Every single one is hard. Having perseverance means, most critically, persevering through failure. I love to talk about my successes, but the only way that I've ever learned anything is through failure."

—Martin Cooper, inventor of the cell phone

Play to your strengths

"When the economy slows down, put your resources where you are strongest. It's tempting to do the opposite—to try and shore up your vulnerable spots. But unless those vulnerable niche activities are extremely large and have great potential, you'll just be throwing good money after bad."

—William F. Miller, former chairman,
Borland Software

Dealing with failure

"How you deal with failure determines part of your success as a leader—not only in your own life, but also in the lives of people around you."

—Kim Clark, former dean,
Harvard Business School

Grow into success

"Failing is one of the best tutors in career development. Consider the story of a new bank president who went to meet his predecessor. Upon being introduced he quickly said, 'I would like to know what have been the keys to your success.' The older man looked at him for a moment and replied, 'Young man, I can sum it up in two words: Good decisions.' To that the young man replied, 'I thank you immensely for that advice, sir, but how does one come to know which are the good decisions?' 'One word, young man,' replied the old man. 'Experience.' 'That's all good and well,' said the young executive, 'but how does one get experience?' 'Two words,' replied the old man. 'Bad decisions.'

"If you really want to succeed, be prepared to grow into it."

—Lou Stoops, pastor and "Monday Motivator,"
Fox television

The success of failure

"We owe our economic development, our form of government, and even our physical existence to spectacular flops."

—P. J. O'Rourke, commentator and
author of *Eat the Rich*

No buts

"Many people begin their criticism with sincere praise followed by the word 'but' and ending with a critical statement. For example, in trying to change a child's careless attitude toward studies, we might say, 'We're really proud of you, Johnnie, for raising your grades this term. But if you had worked harder on your algebra, the results would have been better.'

"In this case, Johnnie might feel encouraged until he heard the word 'but.' . . . To him, the praise seemed only to be a contrived lead-in to a critical inference of failure. . . .

"This could be easily overcome by changing the word 'but' to 'and.' 'We're really proud of you, Johnnie, for raising your grades this term, and by continuing the same conscientious efforts next term, your algebra grade can be up with all the others.'

"Now, Johnnie would accept the praise because there was no follow-up of an inference of failure."

—Dale Carnegie

Success is always relative

"In the end, the strong get stronger, and the weak get weaker.

"That's why as a leader, in good times or in bad, your goal is always the same: to beat the competition. Sales may be sluggish, and profits may be low, but the real issue is, are you doing better than your competitors? Success is always relative."

—Robert Crandall, former chairman and CEO,
American Airlines

That's what (business) friends are for

"It's interesting when you have [a failure], you reach one point where you have a chance of coming out or not coming out of it. If you don't come out, you become what they commonly refer to as a loser. If you do come out of it, it is usually because of the influence someone has on you."

—Bernie Marcus, founder, Home Depot

Reward failure

"We reward failure. I remember some guys came up with a lamp that didn't work, and we gave them all television sets. You have to do it, because otherwise people will be afraid to try things."

—Jack Welch, former chairman and CEO,
General Electric

Great gigs

"You undoubtedly read *Dilbert*. I read *Dilbert*. We laugh at *Dilbert*, and *Dilbert* talks of a world where, fundamentally, the opportunity to create your own shtick doesn't come easy. Workers aren't exactly inundated with projects that would create a signature. But now there is a requirement that you take assignments and bend them in a way that allows you to have something to talk about. Every employee who will survive has to turn projects into stuff that gets the person on the other side of the recruiter's desk excited."

—Tom Peters, author, *WOW!*

SAM WALTON'S 10 RULES FOR SUCCESS

Sam Walton, the founder of Wal-Mart, died April 5, 1992. Just how successful was he?

Here's one way to put his accomplishments into perspective. When *Forbes* magazine did its annual ranking of the world's richest people in 2005, Walton's heirs (sons S. Robson Walton, Jim Walton, John Walton, daughter Alice Walton, and widow Helen) *each* placed within the top 13 spots. They had a combined worth of more than $91 billion, which was more than Bill Gates and Warren Buffett, the men who finished first and second, combined.

Here are Sam Walton's rules for success:

Rule #1. *Commit to your business.* Believe in it more than anything else. If you love your work, you'll be out there every day trying to do the best you can, and pretty soon everybody around will catch the passion from you like a fever.

Rule #2. *Share your profits with all your associates, and treat them as partners.* In turn, they will treat you as a partner, and together you will all perform beyond your wildest expectations.

Rule #3. *Motivate your partners.* Money and ownership aren't enough. Set high goals, encourage competition, and then keep score. Make bets with outrageous payoffs.

Rule #4. *Communicate everything you possibly can to your partners.* The more they know, the more they'll understand. The more they understand, the more they'll care. Once they care, there's no stopping them. Information is power, and the gain you get from empowering your associates more than offsets the risk of informing your competitors.

Rule #5. Appreciate everything your associates do for the business. Nothing else can quite substitute for a few well-chosen, well-timed, sincere words of praise. They're absolutely free and worth a fortune.

Rule #6. Celebrate your success and find humor in your failures. Don't take yourself so seriously. Loosen up and everyone around you will loosen up. Have fun and always show enthusiasm. When all else fails, put on a costume and sing a silly song.

Rule #7. Listen to everyone in your company, and figure out ways to get them talking. The folks on the front line—the ones who actually talk to customers—are the only ones who really know what's going on out there. You'd better find out what they know.

Rule #8. Exceed your customers' expectations. If you do, they'll come back over and over. Give them what they want—and a little more. Let them know you appreciate them. Make good on all your mistakes, and don't make excuses—apologize. Stand behind everything you do. "Satisfaction guaranteed" will make all the difference.

Rule #9. Control your expenses better than your competition. This is where you can always find the competitive advantage. You can make a lot of mistakes and still recover if you run an efficient operation. Or you can be brilliant and still go out of business if you're too inefficient.

Rule #10. Swim upstream. Go the other way. Ignore the conventional wisdom. If everybody is doing it one way, there's a good chance you can find your niche by going exactly in the opposite direction.

CHAPTER 22
The Future

S trong leaders are always optimistic. Sure, they have their bad days. And of course their companies go through rough times. But invariably they are always upbeat when you ask them about the future.

It is easy to dismiss their optimism as Pollyannaish, or say that anyone who can be upbeat when their company is going through a difficult stretch has a tenuous hold on reality. But either assessment is hard to defend.

First, very few delusional people get to run companies. Egoists? Sure. Self-aggrandizers? Sometimes. But people who are delusional? No.

And *Pollyannaish* isn't accurate, either. It's not that these leaders think there will be a happy ending no matter what. It's just that these leaders believe that the future is going to be better than the past has been.

Why?

Because that has always been the case.

Everyone who talks longingly about the "good old days" when they never locked their doors at night, knew their neighbors, and the price of a pack of gum was a nickel always seems to forget that there are still places where people don't lock their doors, you can always know your neighbors, and—with its price adjusted for inflation—that pack of gum still doesn't cost much.

And what the naysayers forget when they talk about how much better life used to be are the medical advances that are increasing life expectancy, the improvements in office and factory productivity, and the technological leaps that are making our lives more convenient. When was the last time you went looking for a pay phone?

The best leaders are optimistic about the future because they have reason to be—and because business is, per se, predicated on the assumption of a future that is better, bigger, faster, and more profitable than today.

A unique moment in history

"We are living at a unique moment in history: Seldom has a society changed so thoroughly, so rapidly. The big challenge for everyone—but especially for older generations—is to accept, rather than resist, the pace of change. Only by embracing change can we mold it in a way that benefits all of us."

—Lewis Jaffe, president and founder,
21st Century Networking

The future calls

"With leaders, the future calls to them in a voice they can't drown out. The future is more real than the present; it compels them to act."

—Marcus Buckingham, author,
The Three Things You Need to Know

A company's worst enemy

"History is a company's worst enemy. To think about the future, you must abandon tradition and convention.... My advice: Understand that there are no guarantees, make a bet on one possible future, and then throw everything you have into it."

—Robert Baldock, president of
EDS Continental Europe

Why pessimists make lousy leaders

"The future is not shaped by people who don't really believe in the future. Men and women of vitality have always been prepared to bet their futures, even their lives, on ventures of unknown outcome. If they had all looked before they leaped, we would still be crouched in caves sketching animal pictures on the wall."

—John W. Gardner, winner of the Presidential Medal of Freedom,
the highest civilian honor in the United States

Profit is like breathing

"It is essential that we preserve our future economically. Profit, like breathing, is indispensable."

—Max DePree, former chairman, Herman Miller

Entrepreneurs everywhere

"We will start to see more entrepreneurs at every level of the organization. The opportunity for individuals to make choices is increasingly driving every aspect of work and life. A move toward more-decentralized networks is good news for individual creativity and productivity."

—Harlan Cleveland, director, World Future Society, and
president emeritus, World Academy of Art and Science

Tomorrow

"No one is less ready for tomorrow than the person who holds the most rigid beliefs about what tomorrow will contain."

—Watts Wacker, consultant and author,
The Deviant's Advantage

The return of emotion

"We are in the twilight of a society based on data. As information and intelligence become the domain of computers, society will place new value on the one human ability that can't be automated: emotion. Imagination, myth, ritual—the language of emotion—will affect everything from our purchasing decisions to how well we work with others."

—Rolf Jensen, director, Copenhagen
Institute for Future Studies

The new world order

"Dumb good-looking people with great parents have been displaced by smart ambitious people with scuffed shoes."

—David Brooks, author, *On Paradise Drive*

Shaping the future

"I believe that we have a much greater capacity to shape the future than we allow ourselves to think."

—Adam Kahane, partner,
Centre for Generative Leadership

We have only just begun

"For the first time in history, technologies allow us to gain the economic benefits of large organizations, like economies of scale and knowledge, without giving up the human benefits of small ones, such as freedom, creativity, motivation and flexibility."

—Thomas W. Malone, professor, Sloan
School of Management, MIT

The revolution

"Be a revolutionary."

—Guy Kawasaki, author, consultant

Progress comes from . . .

"Progress comes from the people who think against the grain. Without nonconformists, you don't advance."

—Saw Ken Wye, managing director,
Microsoft Singapore

Dream it

"If you can dream it, you can do it."

—Walt Disney

Anticipating

"Everyone thinks that the past is uninteresting. It's not hot. It's not new. I love the idea of the future, but the future isn't here yet. If you want to make good decisions about what's to come, look behind you."

—Nathan Myhrvold, former chief
technology officer, Microsoft

Reinvention

"Reinvention. What a quintessential American idea. It's the frontier spirit. It's Ben Franklin. It's Ralph Waldo Emerson, and by God, it's Tony Robbins and Stephen Covey, too. They all understand the American impetus and genius for wholesale self-reinvention. We survive by staring change in the eye—and adapting."

—Tom Peters, management consultant

Mosquito power

"If you think you're too small to have an impact, try going to bed with a mosquito in the room."

—Dame Anita Roddick, founder,
The Body Shop

Sources

1. Change

Allow events to change you. *Fast Company.* 10/2000.

Brick by brick. *Fast Company.* 5/2003.

Change doesn't happen if you don't work at it. *Fast Company.*

Embrace change. *Fast Company.* 3/2002.

The faces that shape change. *The Fifth Discipline,* by Peter Senge. Doubleday/Currency. 1994.

How change doesn't happen. *Fast Company.* 10/2001.

If you don't like change. *Re-imagine: Business Excellence in a Disruptive Age,* by Tom Peters. Dorling Kindersley Publishing. 2003. Epigraph.

The metabolism of change. *Fast Company.* 4/1999.

The more success you achieve, the more difficult it is to change. *Fast Company.* 7–8/1999.

The most effective way to manage change is to create it. *Managing in the Next Society,* by Peter Drucker. Truman Talley Books. 2002.

Never stop looking out the window. *Fast Company.* 5/2001.

Nothing good lasts forever. *Fast Company.* 4/2001.

Only pissed-off people change the world. *Fast Company.* 12/2001.

Persuading. *Fast Company.* 11/2004.

Picture an egg. *The Heart of Change: Real-Life Stories of How People Change Their Organizations,* by John P. Kotter and Dan S. Cohen. Harvard Business School Press. 2002.

The search for facts. *My Years with General Motors*, by Alfred Sloan. Doubleday. 1996.

Speak to people's feelings. *The Heart of Change: Real-Life Stories of How People Change their Organizations*, by John P. Kotter and Dan S. Cohen. Harvard Business School Press. 2002.

There is a good reason people fight change. *Fast Company.* 12/1999.

Why don't companies change? *Fast Company.* 5/2002.

2. Communication

Chief communications officer. *Fast Company.* 9/2003.

Clarity, conviction, and compassion. *Fast Company.* 12/2003.

Face time. *Taking Charge: 236 Proven Principles of Effective Leadership*, by Byrd Baggett. Rutledge Hill Press. 1995.

How to communicate. *Fast Company.* 10/2004.

How to know what is really going on. *301 Great Management Ideas from America's Most Innovative Small Companies.* Edited by Sara P. Noble. Inc. Publishing. 1991.

If you can't listen . . . *Fast Company.* 10/2004.

It's all in the translation. *Fast Company.* 11/1998.

It's impossible to overcommunicate. *Lessons from the Top: The Search for America's Best Business Leaders*, by Thomas J. Neff and James M. Citrin. Doubleday. 1999.

A leader's principal role is communication. *Fast Company.* 8/2005.

Leading well. *Fast Company.* 4/2004.

Listen. *Fast Company.* 4/1999.

PowerPoint isn't writing. *Fast Company.* 4/200.

Providing answers. *Being Direct: Marking Advertising Pay*, by Lester Wunderman. Direct Marketing Association. 2004.

Relevance. *Fast Company.* 11/2003.

Share in all directions. *The Leader in You*, by Dale Carnegie. Pocket. 1995.

They will only speak truth to power if . . . *Leading People: Transforming Business from the Inside Out*, by Robert H. Rosen with Paul B. Brown. Viking. 1996.

Understanding the story. *Fast Company.* 12/2001.

Why repetition works. *Fast Company.* 12/2001.

Words must be linked to deeds. *Fast Company.* 10/2004.

You are the message. *You are the Message: Secrets of Master Communicators,* by Roger Ailes with Jon Kraushar. Dow Jones Irwin. 1988.

3. Creativity and Innovation

Being creative. *Fast Company.* 4/2000.

Brainstorming at ski lodges. *The Art of Innovation: Lessons in Creativity from IDEO, America's Leading Design Firm,* by Tom Kelley. Doubleday/Currency. 2001.

The breakthrough zone. *Fast Company.* 2/2004.

Conventional wisdom. *Fast Company.* 12/2002.

Courage is the journey. *Fast Company.* 7–8/1999.

Creativity by the numbers? *Juice: The Creative Fuel That Drives World-Class Inventors,* by Evan I. Schwartz. Harvard Business School Press. 2004.

Creativity requires discipline. *Fast Company.* 12/2002.

Cubical creativity. *Fast Company.* 4/1999.

Customers can't tell you what they will need. *The Innovator's Dilemma,* by Clayton M. Christensen. Harvard Business School Press. 1997.

Don't underestimate the power of luck. *Fast Company.* 2/2004.

Encourage innovation and edit. *Fast Company.* 2/2004.

"Equilibrium equals death." *Fast Company.* 4/2001.

Genius is. "Edison in His Laboratory" by M. A. Rosanoff. *Harper's.* 9/1932.

Getting used to newness. *Fast Company.* 9/2002.

Great ideas have three key elements. *Fast Company.* 3/2004.

An idea is just an idea *Fast Company.* 4/2000.

In the age of the idea. *Fast Company.* 12/1998.

Innovation is a management function. *Making Innovation Work: How to Manage It, Measure It, and Profit from It,* by Tony Davila, Marc Epstein, and Robert Shelton. Wharton Publishing. 2005.

Innovation is relative. *Fast Company.* 7/2001.

Innovation is not an event. *Fast Company.* 4/2003.

The keys to innovation. *Fast Company.* 4/2000.

No straight lines. *Fast Company.* 11/1998.

Outside the box. *Esquire.* 1/2004.

Pay attention to ideas. *Fast Company*. 1/2000.

Prerequisites of innovation. *Fast Company*. 4/2000.

Radical innovation. *Fast Company*. 5/2003.

Show me the results. *Fast Company*. 1/2001.

Show you care about new ideas. *Fast Company*. 1–2/2000.

Stuck. *Fast Company*. 6/2004.

The "rules" for innovation. *Fast Company*. 12/2004.

A new environment. *Fast Company*. 11/2002.

What artists do. *Marketing Masters: Lessons in the Art of Marketing*, by Paul B. Brown. Harper & Row. 1988.

4. Customer Service

Customer retention. *Be Our Guest: Perfecting the Art of Customer Service*, by the Disney Institute. Disney Editions. 2003.

Consistency. *Hug Your Customers: The Proven Way to Personalize Sales*, by Jack Mitchell. Hyperion. 2003.

Customer service is your job. *Quality Customer Service: How to Win with the Customer*, by William B. Martin. Crisp Publications (Fourth Edition). 2000.

Do you know what customers want? *Fast Company*. 10/2004.

Don't hesitate. *Customers for Life*, by Carl Sewell and Paul B. Brown. Doubleday. 2002 (Revised and updated edition.) 2002.

The most important person in the world? *Customer Satisfaction Is Worthless, Customer Loyalty Is Priceless: How to Make Customers Love You, Keep Them Coming Back and Tell Everyone They Know*, by Jeffrey Gitomer. Bard Press. 1998.

Moments of truth. *Moments of Truth*, by Jan Carlson. Ballinger. 1987.

The one secret to giving great service. *Fast Company*. 5/2001.

The real cost of cost reduction. *Passionate and Profitable*, by Lior Arussy. Wiley. 2005.

Selling is not about peddling a product. *Fast Company*. 11/1998.

The source of competitive advantage. *Building Great Customer Experiences*, by Colin Shaw. Palgrave. 2002.

There is always something you can improve. *Fast Company*. 12/2000.

You are the company. *Knock Your Socks Off Customer Service*, by Ron Zemke. Amacom. 1991.

You can't give away the store. *Super Service: Seven Keys to Delivering Great*

Customer Service . . . Even When You Don't Feel Like It! . . . Even When They Don't Deserve It!, by Jeff Gee, Val Gee. McGraw-Hill. 1999.

You can't give service if . . . Creating Customer Evangelists: How Loyal Customers Become a Volunteer Sales Force, by Ben McConnell. Dearborn. 2002.

Where business is won or lost. Fast Company. 10/2004.

5. Decision Making

Debating is easy. Fast Company. 10/1998.

Decisions by themselves are meaningless. Fast Company. 6/2000.

How to make a decision. Winning Decisions: Getting It Right the First Time, by J. Edward Russo and Paul J.H. Schoemaker. Doubleday. 2001.

How to make better decisions. Fast Company. 10/2002.

Intelligent compromises. Fast Company. 11/1999.

Intuition. Fast Company. 12/1999.

Intuition will lead you astray. Fast Company. 10/1998.

The invisible hand. The Wealth of Nations, by Adam Smith. Bantam Classics. 2003.

Just-in-time decisions. Fast Company. 10/1998.

Learning from experience. Fast Company. 11/2002.

Provide context. Fast Company. 3/2000.

Trust your gut. Baby and Child Care, by Dr. Benjamin Spock. Pocket Books. 8th edition. 2004.

Try not to make decisions for others. Fast Company. 10/1998.

Use your intuition. Intuition at Work: Why Developing Your Gut Instincts Will Make You Better at What You Do, by Gary Klein. Doubleday. 2003.

The way to bet. This is attributed to American journalist and author Damon Runyon, who was paraphrasing the Bible, specifically Ecclesiastes 9:11: "I returned, and saw under the sun, that the race is not to the swift, nor the battle to the strong, neither yet bread to the wise, nor yet riches to men of understanding, nor yet favor to men of skill; but time and chance happeneth to them all."

When your intuition is out of sync with analysis. Fast Company. 10/1998.

Why meetings are ineffective. Death by Meeting: A Leadership Fable . . . About Solving the Most Painful Problem in Business, by Patrick M. Lencioni. Jossey-Bass. 2004.

You must make money. Fast Company. 7/2001.

6. Welcome to the Design Revolution

Attractive things work better. Emotional Design: Why We Love (or Hate) Everyday Things, by Donald A. Norman. Basic Books. 2004.

Becoming a design leader. The Art of Innovation: Lessons in Creativity from IDEO, America's Leading Design Firm, by Tom Kelley. Doubleday/Currency. 2001.

Breaking through the clutter. The Substance of Style: How the Rise of Aesthetic Value Is Remaking Commerce, Culture, and Consciousness, by Virginia Postrel. HarperCollins. 2003.

Customers appreciate good design. Fast Company. 06/2005.

Design for profit. The Profit Zone: How Strategic Business Design Will Lead You to Tomorrow's Profits, by Adrian Slywotzky, David J. Morrison and Bob Andelman. Three Rivers Press. 2002.

Design isn't an abstraction. Fast Company. 12/2000.

Developing great products. Creating Breakthrough Products: Innovation from Product Planning to Program Approval, by Jonathan Cagan and Craig M. Vogel. Financial Times/Prentice Hall. 2002.

An enterprise's most important asset. Fast Company. 6/2004.

Form is function. Fast Company. 10/1999.

Getting the organization to accept the importance of design. Fast Company. 12/2004.

Good design is good business. Fast Company. 6/2004.

Grow your own idea. Fast Company. 6/2004.

How to design an office. Designs for Living, by Malcolm Gladwell. The New Yorker. 12/2000.

The highest calling. The Rise of the Creative Class: And How It's Transforming Work, Leisure, Community and Everyday Life, by Richard Florida. Basic Books. (Reprint edition). 2004.

98 percent common sense. Fast Company. 10/1999.

Sifting through sand for seashells. The Elements of Graphic Design: Space, Unity, Page Architecture, and Type, by Alexander W. White. Watson-Guptill Publications. 2002.

Show the future. Fast Company. 6/2004.

A voice at the table. Fast Company. 12/2004.

7. Execute!

Be ruthless. *Fast Company Online*, 1/1995.

Doing good is good business. *Fast Company*. 8/2002.

Execution is . . . *Execution: The Discipline of Getting Things Done*, by Larry Bossidy and Ram Charan. Crown. 2002.

Execution beats strategy every time. Speech as part of the Dean's Lecture Series at the Jesse H. Jones Graduate School of Management. Rice University. 1/2003.

Execution for Dummies. *It's Not What You Say . . . It's What You Do: How Following Through at Every Level Can Make or Break Your Company.* Laurence Haughton. Doubleday/Currency. 2005.

Faster, cheaper better. *Fast Company*. 11/2002.

Focus. *Execution Plain and Simple: Twelve Steps to Achieving Any Goal on Time and on Budget*, by Robert A. Neiman. McGraw Hill. 2004.

Follow up on everything. *Patton's One-Minute Messages: Tactical Leadership Skills of Business Managers*, by Charles Province. Presidio Press. 1995.

Just do it. Salesstar.com. Posted 3/15/2004

Knowing isn't the same as doing. *Fast Company*. 6/2000.

Never disappoint your customers. Vol. 81, No. 7, *Harvard Business Review*, July 2003. Nitin is a professor at Harvard Business School. William Joyce is a professor of strategy and organizational theory at Dartmouth College's Tuck School of Business. Bruce Roberson is executive vice president of marketing and sales at Safety-Kleen.

The next steps. *The Art and Discipline of Strategic Leadership*, by Mike Freedman. McGraw-Hill. 2002.

Optimism can't outweigh expectations. *Fast Company*. 3/2004.

When excellent execution does not matter. *The Toyota Way: 14 Management Principles from the World's Greatest Manufacturer*, by Jeffrey Liker. McGraw-Hill. 2003.

8. Hiring *and* Developing *and* Retaining Great Employees

Build on what they do best. *Fast Company*. 9/2000.

Chemistry is important. *Fast Company*. 7/2002.

Concern costs nothing. *The Corporate Coach,* by James B. Miller with Paul B. Brown. HarperCollins. 1984.

Concentrate of the stars. *Only the Paranoid Survive,* by Andrew S. Grove. Currency, 1996.

Good people are in short supply. *Fast Company.* 1–2/2000.

Have your best do the hiring. *Fast Company.* 6/1999.

How to be successful dealing with people. *Fast Company.* 6/2002.

Hire right. *Fast Company.* 8/2004.

If something doesn't comply? *Fast Company.* 3/2001.

Invest in people. *Fast Company.* 12/1999.

An invisible sign. *The Corporate Coach,* by James B. Miller with Paul B. Brown. HarperCollins. 1984.

Mentoring is demeaning. *Fast Company.* 10/2003.

A never-ending journey. *Fast Company.* 10/2003.

No bozos. *How Would You Move Mount Fuji?: Microsoft's Cult of the Puzzle—How the World's Smartest Companies Select the Most Creative Thinkers,* by William Poundstone. Little Brown. 2004.

A pipeline of talent. *Fast Company.* 1/2001.

People basically do what they want to do. Larry Bossidy in a conversation with Paul B. Brown. 2002

Recruiting is everybody's job. *Fast Company.* 12/1999.

Say thank you. *Fast Company.* 1/2005.

Stop trying to change people. *Fast Company.* 8/2001.

Talent. *Fast Company.* 12/2002.

There are no limits. *Made in America,* by Sam Walton with John Huey. Doubleday, 1992.

Understand what is behind every employee complaint. *Fast Company.* 5/2001.

The unequal treatment of equals. *Fast Company.* 3/2005.

You are only as good as your people. *Fast Company.* 1/2001.

You can't compromise. *Fast Company.* 7/2001.

Give direction, not criticism. *Fast Company.* 7/2001.

You've got to give people a voice. *301 Great Management Ideas from America's Most Innovative Small Companies.* Edited by Sara P. Noble. Inc. Publishing. 1991.

9. Technology Is Not a Strategy

Customer driven. Building Trust: Leading CEOs Speak Out: How They Create It, Strengthen It, and Sustain It. Arthur W. Page Society. 2004.

The CIO must take a leading role. The New CIO Leader: Setting the Agenda and Delivering Results, by Marianne Broadbent, Ellen Kitzis. Harvard Business Review. 2004.

The differentiator. Business @ the Speed of Thought, by Bill Gates. Warner Business Books. 5/2000.

IT is a commodity. Does IT Matter? Information Technology and the Corrosion of Competitive Advantage?, by Nicholas G. Carr. Harvard Business School Press. 2004.

Managing IT. Managing IT as a Business : A Survival Guide for CEOs, by Mark Lutchen. Wiley. 2003.

Managing something original. Juice: The Creative Fuel That Drives World-Class Inventors, by Evan I. Schwartz. Harvard Business School Press. 2004.

Reassembling knowledge. Fast Company. 10/2000.

The servant of the people. Leading People: Transforming Business from the Inside Out, by Robert H. Rosen with Paul B. Brown. Viking. 1996.

Technology trends. The Map of Innovation: Creating Something Out of Nothing, by Kevin O'Connor with Paul B. Brown. Crown. 2003.

Want better IT? Don't have IT run it. IT Governance: How Top Performers Manage IT Decision Rights for Superior Results, by Peter Weill and Jeanne W. Ross. Harvard Business School Press. 2004.

What the CIO must do. The New CIO Leader: Setting the Agenda and Delivering Results, by Marianne Broadbent and Ellen Kitzis, Harvard Business School Press. 2004.

Why IT projects fail. Revolutionizing IT: The Art of Managing Information Technology Effectively, by David Andrews and Kenneth Johnson. Wiley. 2002.

10. Knowledge

Competing in the global economy. Speech by Kenneth T. Derr, chairman and chief executive officer, Chevron Corporation, to the

American Productivity & Quality Center's Knowledge Imperative Symposium. Houston, Texas. September 11, 1995.

Everything can be traced back to the same source. *What's So New About the New Economy?* Harvard Business Review. 1–2/1993.

Knowledge management. *The Complete Idiot's Guide to Knowledge Management,* by Melissie Clemmons Rumizen. Penguin. 2001.

Knowledge is . . . *Working Knowledge,* by Thomas H. Davenport, Laurence Prusak. Project Management Institute. 1997.

Knowledge is an infinite. *The New Knowledge Management : Complexity, Learning, and Sustainable Innovation,* by Mark W. McElroy. Butterworth-Heinemann. 2002.

Best practices. *Gonzo Marketing: Winning Through Worst Practices,* by Christopher Locke. Perseus. 2002.

The only new thing. *Plain Speaking: An Oral History of Harry S Truman.* Putnam. 1974.

Putting knowledge to work. *Enabling Knowledge Creation: How to Unlock the Mystery of Tacit Knowledge and Release the Power of Innovation,* by Georg Von Krogh. Oxford University Press. 2000.

Take time to reflect. *Fast Company.* 9/2001.

Translating experience into knowledge. *Common Knowledge: How Companies Thrive by Sharing What They Know,* by Nancy M. Dixon. Harvard Business School Press. 2000.

20 percent. *Intellectual Capital: The New Wealth of Organizations,* by Thomas A. Stewart. Doubleday/Currency. 1997.

We need more oops! Lots of CEOs have sort of said this. And many have acted on it, by actually rewarding failures. However, we will take full credit for creating the (pending) bumper sticker.

Where are our assets? *The Trouble with Advertising,* by John O'Toole. Chelsea House. 1981.

You must remember this. *Deep Smarts: How to Cultivate and Transfer Enduring Business Wisdom,* by Dorothy Leonard and Walter Swap. Harvard Business School Press. 2004. And *Lost Knowledge: Confronting the Threat of an Aging Workforce.* Oxford University Press. 2004.

You are competing based on the knowledge of your employees. *If Only We Knew What We Know: The Transfer of Internal Knowledge and Best Practice,* by Carla O'Dell, C. Jackson Grayson. Free Press. 1998.

11. Leadership

Be curious. *Fast Company.* 7/2004.

The CEO is not Superman. *Fast Company.* 8/2001.

The challenges of leadership . . . *Fast Company.* 6/1999.

Changing minds. *Changing Minds: The Art and Science of Changing Our Own and Other People's Minds,* by Howard Gardner. Harvard Business School Press. 2004.

The difference between a manager and a leader. *Learning to Lead* (Third Edition), by Warren Bennis and Joan Goldsmith. Basic Books. 2003.

Focus. *Fast Company.* 12/2001.

Give direction. *Leading Up: How to Lead Your Boss So You Both Win,* by Michael Useem. Three River Press. 2003.

Growing your people. *Jack Welch & The G.E. Way: Management Insights and Leadership Secrets of the Legendary CEO,* by Robert B. Slater. McGraw-Hill. 1998.

If you go broke, you can't take care of anyone. *Customers for Life: How to Turn a One-Time Buyer into a Lifetime Customer,* by Carl Sewell and Paul B. Brown. Doubleday. 2002. (Revised edition.)

Emotional and intellectual anchors. *Fast Company.* 8/2001.

Leaders develop other leaders. *Fast Company.* 8/2003.

Leadership is about responsibility. *Fast Company.* 9/2003.

Listening to the voice of David. *Fast Company.* 7/2003.

A noble cause. *Built to Last* (10th anniversary edition.), by Jim Collins and Jerry I. Porras. HarperBusiness. 2005.

The people in the trenches. *Fast Company.* 6/2003.

Persuasion, conciliation, and patience. *The Ordeal of Power: A Political Memoir of the Eisenhower Years,* by Emmett John Hughes. Athenaeum. 1963.

The primal job of leadership is emotional. *Primal Leadership: Realizing the Power of Emotional Intelligence,* by Daniel Goleman, Rickard Boyatzis and Annie McKee. Harvard Business School Press. 2002.

Roll up your sleeves. *Dig Your Well Before You Are Thirsty,* by Harvey MacKay. Currency. 1997.

Teaching. *Fast Company.* 6/2003.

Say thank you. *Leadership Is an Art*, by Max De Pree. Doubleday/ Currency. 1989.

Servant leadership. *Fast Company*. 10/2004.

Simplify. *Fast Company*. 3/2000.

To be a leader. *Fast Company*. 1/2002.

Toxic leaders. *Fast Company*. 11/2004.

Truly caring. *The Carolina Way: Leadership Lessons from a Life in Coaching*, by Dean Smith. Penguin. 2004.

Vision. *Fast Company*. 3/2001.

Well thought out. *Execution Plain and Simple: Twelve Steps to Achieving Any Goal on Time and on Budget*, by Robert A. Neiman. McGraw-Hill. 2004.

What leaders don't do. *Fast Company*. 10/2002.

What I learned at West Point. *Fast Company*. 6/2001.

Tyranny. *Fast Company*. 6/1999.

You can't create a leader in a classroom. *Fast Company*. 11/2000.

Your power is in your people. *Leading People: Transforming Business from the Inside Out*, by Robert H. Rosen with Paul B. Brown. Viking. 1996.

"We have to talk." *Fast Company*. 7/2004.

12. Life and Career

Appealing. *Fast Company*. 2/2003.

Balance. *The Seven-Day Weekend: Changing the Way Work Works*, by Ricardo Semler. Portfolio. 2004.

Balance is bunk. *Fast Company*. 10/2004.

Be a spin doctor. *Fast Company*. 6/2004.

Do what you love. This is said during 31% of all commencement addresses. The quote is also the title of a book written by Marsha Sinetar. Dell. 1989.

The 8th habit. *The 8th Habit: From Effectiveness to Greatness*, by Stephen R. Covey. Free Press. 2004.

Every second counts. *Fast Company*. 11/1999.

Finding job satisfaction in the work itself. *Fast Company*. 9/1999.

The Golden Rule. What is so intriguing is that The Golden Rule can be found in just about every religion.

How to build your career. *Fast Company*. 6/2004.

The things that matter most. *Fast Company.* 2/2005.

Keep looking. *Fast Company.* 10/2005.

Lateral moves. *Fast Company.* 12/2004.

Passing through the fire. A speech Gardner gave at Stanford, where he was once a professor. http://www.jonandgail.com/jwork/GardnerSpeech.php.

Looking smart. *The Dilbert Principle,* by Scott Adams. HarperBusiness. 1997.

Love what you do? *Lessons from the Top: The Search for America's Best Business Leaders,* by Thomas J. Neff and James M. Citrin. Doubleday. 1999.

More than a job. *Leadership on the Line: Staying Alive Through the Dangers of Leading,* by Ronald A. Heifetz and Marty Linsky. Harvard Business School Press. 2002.

No entitlements. *The Success Principles,* by Jack Canfield with Janet Switzer. HarperCollins. 2005.

Only you can stop you. *See You at the Top* (25th Anniversary edition), by Zig Ziglar. Pelican. 2000.

The 7 habits of effective people. *The 7 Habits of Highly Effective People,* by Stephen R. Covey. Free Press. 1989.

Think about what is worthwhile. *Fast Company.* 3/2001.

Suck it up. *Fast Company.* 4/1999.

Time, time, time is on your side. *A Bias for Action,* by Heike Bruch and Sumantra Ghoshal. Harvard Business School Press. 2004. *Leave the Office Earlier,* by Laura Stack. Broadway Books. 2004. *Leverage Your Best, Ditch the Rest,* by Scott Blanchard and Madeline Homan. William Morrow. 2004. *Organized for Success: Top Executives and CEOs Reveal the Organizing Principles That Helped Them Reach the Top,* by Stephanie Winston. Crown. 2004.

Unhappy bedfellows. *Creative Company: How St. Luke's Became "the Ad Agency to End All Ad Agencies,"* by Andy Law. Wiley. 1999.

You own your career. *Fast Company.* 12/1998.

Your inner voice. *Fast Company.* 9/2004.

Waste not, want not. *Fast Company.* 8/2004.

What should I do with my life, aka The Question. *Fast Company.* 1/2003.

13. Managing

The art of human relationships. How to Win Friends and Influence People, by Dale Carnegie. (He was quoting a conversation with Henry Ford.) Pocket (Reissue edition.) 1990.

The best people you can find. The Fall of the Berlin Wall: Reassessing the Causes and Consequences of the Cold War. Peter Schweizer (Editor) Hoover Institution Press. 2000.

Confidence. The First-Time Manager, by Loren B. Belker. Amacom. 1997.

Crisis Management. Why Some Companies Emerge Stronger and Better from a Crisis, by Ian I. Mitroff. Amacom. 2005.

Don't try to change people. Fast Company. 9/2000.

The empowering manager. Just Promoted: How to Survive and Thrive in Your First 12 Months as a Manager, by Edward H. Betof. McGraw-Hill. 1992.

Face the problem head-on. Who Says Elephants Can't Dance? Inside IBM's Historic Turnaround, by Louis V. Gerstner, Jr. HarperBusiness. 2002.

The flywheel effect. Fast Company. 10/2001.

How to be a great coach. Fast Company. 12/1998.

If the line manager is not innovating . . . Fast Company. 5/1999.

It is nice if they like you, but . . . Monday Morning Leadership, by David Cottrell. Cornerstone Leadership Institute. 2002.

The long-term good. Enterprise Risk Management: From Incentives to Controls, by James Lam. Wiley. 2003.

Manage, don't lead. Fast Company. 3/2005.

Managers must juggle. Becoming a Manager: How New Managers Master the Challenges of Leadership, by Linda A. Hill. Harvard Business School Press. 2003.

People who feel good about themselves. The One Minute Manager, by Kenneth Blanchard. William Morrow. (10th anniversary edition) 1983.

Put down the whip. Lessons from the Top: The Search for America's Best Business Leaders, by Thomas J. Neff and James M. Citrin. Doubleday. 1999.

Recognition. How Full Is Your Bucket? Positive Strategies for Work and Life, by Tom Rath and Donald O. Clifton. Gallup Press. 2004.

The right to make mistakes. How to Be a Manager: A Practical Guide to Tips and Techniques, by Robert W. Gallant. Lewis Publishers. 1991.

Tired ears. *Fast Company.* 2/2005.

Weak managers never say I don't know. 13 *Fatal Errors Managers Make and How You Can Avoid Them,* by W. Steven Brown. Berkley Publishing. (Reprint edition) 1995.

What gets done. *Landmarks of Tomorrow: A Report on the New "Post-Modern" World,* by Peter F. Drucker. Harper & Row. 1959.

Why managers are failing. Interview with Ram Charan conducted by Paul B. Brown.

14. Marketing

The acid test. 301 *Great Management Ideas from America's Most Innovative Small Companies.* Edited by Sara P. Noble. Inc. Publishing. 1991.

Boring always fails. *Fast Company.* 2/2003.

Creating a customer. *Innovation and Entrepreneurship: Practice and Principles,* by Peter F. Drucker. HarperCollins 1985.

Creating a customer-focused organization. *Customer Mania!,* by Ken Blanchard, Jim Ballard and Fred Finch. Free Press. 2004.

The customer decides what is important. *Fast Company.* 12/1999.

Differentiate. *Fast Company.* 9/1999.

The essence of selling. *Fast Company.* 11/2002.

Fresh and relevant. *Fast Company.* 4/2003.

Get a greater share of your customer's wallet. Adapted from *Customers for Life: How to Turn That One-time Buyer into a Lifetime Customer,* by Carl Sewell and Paul B. Brown. Doubleday/Currency. 2002.

A good match. *Fast Company.* 11/1998.

How to succeed in advertising. Quoted in Stephen Fox's *The Mirror Makers: A History of American Advertising and Its Creators.* William Morrow. 1984.

L.L.'s Golden Rule. The L. L. Bean website. (http://www.llbean.com/ customerService/aboutLLBean/golden_rule.html).

Marketing that does not suck. *Your Marketing Sucks,* by Mark Stevens. Crown. 2003.

Memorable service. *Fast Company.* 9/2001.

Numbers can only tell you so much. *Marketing Masters: Lessons in the Art of Marketing,* by Paul B. Brown. Harper & Row. 1988.

Sell satisfaction. *Fast Company.* 11/1998.

Selling. *Where the Suckers Moon: An Advertising Story,* by Randall Rothenberg. Alfred A. Knopf. 1994.

The three rules of advertising. *Fast Company.* 11/2004.

What people want. *Think Like Your Customers,* by Bill Stinnett. McGraw-Hill. 2004.

When advertising doesn't work. *Fast Company.* 4/2002.

When they don't care. *Esquire.* 1/2005.

Who is the moron? *Confessions of an Advertising Man.* by David Ogilvy. Ballantine. 1971.

Who's the boss? *Fast Company.* 10/2001.

Wow. *Fast Company.* 5/2002.

15. The Organization and Corporate Culture

Auditioning the right people. *Fast Company,* 5/2004.

Being highly effective. *The 8th Habit: From Effectiveness to Greatness,* by Stephen R. Covey. Free Press. 2004.

Building a strong culture. *Fast Company.* 7/2002.

Constructively dissatisfied. *Fast Company.* 9/2005.

The lessons that workers learn. *Fast Company.* 3/2002.

Different. *Fast Company.* 7/2000.

Faith in the value of human potential. *Fast Company.* 10/1998.

Flexibility. *Fast Company.* 3/2002.

Focusing outward. *Lessons from the Top: The Search for America's Best Business Leaders,* by Thomas J. Neff and James M. Citrin. Doubleday. 1999.

The fundamentals of business. Speech as part of the Dean's Lecture Series at the Jesse H. Jones Graduate School of Management. Rice University. 1/2003.

Getting sloppy. *Fast Company.* 5/2004.

Has anything really changed? *Organizations: Behavior, Structure, Processes,* by James L. Gibson. Irwin Professional Publishing; 10th edition. 2000.

Is diversity a priority? *Fast Company.* 9/2002.

The language of business. *The Corporation: The Pathological Pursuit of Profit and Power,* by Joel Bakan. Free Press. 2004.

Let people think! *Fast Company.* 5/2002.

Masochists and sadists. *Fast Company.* 1/2003.

The most powerful force in business. *Fast Company.* 2/2002.

Muda. *Lean Thinking: Banish Waste and Create Wealth in Your Corporation,* Revised and Updated, by James P. Womack, Daniel T. Jones. Free Press. 2003.

No wealth without ideas. *Fast Company.* 9/2003.

An organization is . . . *Organizations: Behavior, Structure, Processes,* by James L. Gibson. Irwin Professional Pub.; 10th edition. 2000.

Organizational learning. *Fast Company.* 2/2005.

Profitable growth. *Beyond the Core: Expand Your Market Without Abandoning Your Roots,* Chris Zook. Harvard Business School Press. 2004.

The right goal. If you are not profitable, nothing else matters. *Fast Company.* 3/2001.

Silos. *Fast Company.* 11/2004.

Why meetings are boring. *Death by Meeting: A Leadership Fable. . . About Solving the Most Painful Problem in Business,* by Patrick M. Lencioni. Jossey-Bass. 2004.

16. Teamwork and Partnerships

Acting developmentally. *The Extraordinary Leader: Turning Good Managers into Great Leaders.* John H. Zenger. McGraw-Hill. 2002.

Be flexible. *Fast Company.* 9/1998.

Being at ease. *Fast Company.* 11/2000.

The best in people. *Fast Company.* 4/2004.

Check your ego at the door. *Fast Company.* 4/2002.

Consensus. *Fast Company.* 7/2003.

Every person is very important. *Fast Company.* 4/2000.

The four things that characterize great teams. *Fast Company.* 11/2000.

Goals. *The Corporate Coach,* by James B. Miller with Paul B. Brown. HarperCollins. 1984.

How to build a team. *You Don't Have to Do It Alone: How to Involve Others to Get Things Done,* by Richard H. Axelrod, Emily M. Axelrod, Julie Beedon and Robert W. Jacobs. Berrett-Koehler. 2004.

Human capital. *Future Work,* by Stan Davis and Christopher Meyer. Harvard Business School Press. 2000.

Improvisation. *Fast Company.* 6/2003.

Is it a team, or organizational politics? *Fast Company.* 11/2004.

Leading Up. *Fast Company.* 11/2001.

Lessons from the Hardwood. *The Carolina Way: Leadership Lessons from a Life in Coaching,* by Dean Smith. Penguin. 2004.

Negative energy. *Fast Company.* 11/2000.

None of us is as smart as all of us. *The One Minute Manager,* by Ken Blanchard and Spencer Johnson. William Morrow (Anniversary Edition). 1982.

Partnering. *The Power of We: Succeeding Through Partnerships,* by Jonathan Tisch. John Wiley & Sons. 2004.

Project Management 101. *Working at Warp Speed: The New Rules for Project Success in a Sped-up World,* by Barry Flicker. Berrett-Koehler. 2002.

Servant Leadeship. *Fast Company.* 11/2000.

A successful team? *Fast Company.* 11/2000.

The two-pizza rule. *Fast Company.* 8/2004.

You can't do it alone. *Pushing the Envelope,* by Harvey MacKay. Ballantine Books. 1999.

You need more diversity than you can imagine. *Fast Company.* 2/2001.

Working together. *Fast Company.* 4/2000.

17. Risk

Confront reality. *The Prince,* by Niccolo' Machiavelli. Bantam. Reissue edition. 1984.

Don't be so quick to start a business. *Fast Company.com.* 5/2001.

Don't compound the problem. *Enterprise Risk Management: From Incentives to Controls,* by James Lam. Wiley. 2003.

Every decision involves risk. *Fast Company.* 10/1998.

The fates, the gods, or ourselves. *Against the Gods: The Remarkable Story of Risk,* by Peter Bernstein. Wiley. 1996.

Leave a big leagacy. *Esquire.* 1/2004.

No one person. *Fast Company.* 2/2005.

Paranoia. *Only the Paranoid Survive: How to Exploit the Crisis Points that Challenge Every Business,* by Andrew S. Grove. Doubleday. 1999.

The past is not prologue. *Fast Company.* 7/1999.

Risk at its core. Risk: A Practical Guide for Deciding What's Really Safe and What's Really Dangerous in the World Around You, by David Ropeik. Houghton Mifflin. 2002.

Risk is not a four-letter word. Fast Company. 4/2002.

Set an example. Jack Welch. http://www.msnbc.msn.com/id/7304559/site/newsweek. 2005.

Ten reasons we are going to go out of business. Fast Company. 2/2001.

Test. Fast Company. 6/2000.

We live in a dangerous world. Risk: A Practical Guide for Deciding What's Really Safe and What's Really Dangerous in the World Around You, by David Ropeik. Houghton Mifflin. 2002.

18. Social Responsibility, Trust, and Ethics

The avenues to express greed. Testimony before the U.S. Senate. July 16, 2002.

Be completely forthright. Fast Company. 10/1998.

Courage. Fast Company. 9/2004.

An economic incentive. Fast Company. 1/2004.

For trust to take hold. Learning to Lead (Third Edition), by Warren Bennis and Joan Goldsmith. Basic Books. 2003.

Good business. Remarks made by Commissioner Roel C. Compos at the U.S. Securities and Exchange Commission Open Meeting Regarding Corporate Ethical Behavior in Washington. D.C. 10/2002. http://www.sec.gov/news/speech/spch593.htm.

A good corporate citizen. Fast Company. 1/2004.

Growing a substantial economy. Fast Company. 1/2004.

How would my actions appear. Customers for Life: How to Turn a One-time Buyer into a Lifetime Customer, by Carl Sewell and Paul B. Brown. Doubleday 2002. (Revised edition.)

Integrity transcends borders. Building Trust: Leading CEOs Speak Out: How They Create It, Strengthen It, and Sustain It. Arthur W. Page Society. 2004.

Intent. Building Trust: Leading CEOs Speak Out: How They Create It, Strengthen It, and Sustain It. Arthur W. Page Society. 2004.

Intimacy. Fast Company. 8/2000.

The less we make, the less we have to give away. Fast Company. 8/2000.

No trust, no deal. Building Reputation Capital, by Kevin T. Jackson. Oxford University Press. 2004.

The power of truth. Fast Company. 1/2003.

Trust your associates. Leading People: Transforming Business from the Inside Out, by Robert H. Rosen with Paul B. Brown. Viking. 1996.

Trust your employees. Fast Company. 7/2004.

Two-way communication. Building Trust: Leading CEOs Speak Out: How They Create It, Strengthen It, and Sustain It. Arthur W. Page Society. 2004.

You can't teach honesty. Fast Company. 3/2003.

The worst crime. The Samuel Gompers Papers Volume 6: The American Federation of Labor and the Rise of Progressivism 1902-8, by Stuart B. Kaufman, Peter J. Albert, and Grace Palladino. University of Illinois Press. 1997.

Worse than no policy at all. Remarks made by Commissioner Roel C. Campos at the U.S. Securities and Exchange Commission Open Meeting Regarding Corporate Ethical Behavior in Washington. D.C. October, 2002. http://www.sec.gov/news/speech/spch593.htm.

19. Speed

The acceleration trap. A Bias for Action: How Effective Managers Harness Their Willpower, Achieve Results, and Stop Wasting Time, by Heike Bruch and Sumantra Ghoshal. Harvard Business School Press. 2004.

Catalyst. First, Break All the Rules: What the World's Greatest Managers Do Differently, by Marcus Buckingham and Curt Coffman. Simon & Schuster. 1999.

Do the things that will allow you to be fast. Fast Company. 5/2000.

Do it right. Fast Company. 3/2004.

Fast teams need clear goals. Fast Company. 5/2000.

Faster. Business @ the Speed of Thought: Succeeding in the Digital Economy, by Bill Gates. Warner Business Books. 2000.

First mover advantage. Sydney Finkelstein. Adapted from The Handbook of Business Strategy. ED Media Group. 2002.

First off the mark wins. Fast Company. 5/2000.

How to be fast. Fast Company. 11/2004.

Over-satisfying your customers. The Innovator's Dilemma, by Clayton M. Christensen. HarperBusiness. 2003.

Some things should not be accelerated. In Praise of Slowness: How A

Worldwide Movement Is Challenging the Cult of Speed, by Carl Honore. HarperSanFrancisco. 2004.

Speed kills. *Unleashing the Ideavirus*, by Seth Godin. Hyperion. 2001.

What everyone in the organization must know. *It's Not the Big That Eat the Small . . . It's the Fast That Eat the Slow: How to Use Speed as a Competitive Tool in Business*, by Jason Jennings and Laurence Haughton. Harper Business 2002.

20. Strategy and Growth

Audaciousness. *Fast Company.* 9/2004.

Authorship. *Lessons from the Top: The Search for America's Best Business Leaders*, by Thomas J. Neff and James M. Citrin. Doubleday. 1999.

The basics of commerce. *Fast Company.* 3/2001.

Change from the top. *Fast Company.* 5/1999.

Do it! *Fast Company.* 8/2001.

Don't be a prisoner of your business model. *Fast Company.* 5/2004.

Embracing outrageous goals. *How Great Companies Set Outrageous Objectives and Achieve Them*, Bill Davidson. Wiley. 2003.

Greed is good. *The Wealth of Nations*, by Adam Smith. Bantam Classics. 2003.

How can you be put out of business. *Fast Company.* 2004.

Keep moving. *Harvard Business Review*, by George Start Jr. 7–8/1988.

A management top 10 list. *The Company of Tomorrow: How the Communications Revolution Is Changing Management*, by Frances Cairncross. Harvard Business School Press. 2/2002.

Overcome obstacles. *See You at the Top* (25th Anniversary edition), by Zig Ziglar. Pelican. 2000.

Shoot first. *The Washington Post.* July 28, 2002.

Stay loose. *Fast Company.* 9/1999.

A good strategic plan. *The Art of the Strategist*, by William A. Cohen. Amacom Books. 2004.

Timing. *Fast Company.* 10/2004.

Visionaries. *Fast Company.* 9/2004.

You don't have to be first. *Fast Second: How Smart Companies Bypass Radical Innovation to Enter and Dominate New Markets*, by Constantinos C. Markides and Paul A. Geroski. Jossey-Bass. 2004.

Warriors don't make good CEOs. *Fast Company.* 6/1999.

What strategy is. *Fast Company.* 3/2001.

Win, place, or don't show. *Jack: Straight from the Gut,* by Jack Welch with John A. Byrne. Warner Business Books. 2001.

Winning with ideas. *Fast Company.* 8/2004.

Why we handle difficult problems so badly. *Marketing Masters: Lessons in the Art of Marketing,* by Paul B. Brown. Harper and Row. 1988.

21. The Link Between Success and Failure

Becoming stronger. *Fast Company.* 12/1998.

Boring your way to success. *We Got Fired and It Is the Best Thing That Ever Happened to Us,* by Harvey MacKay. Ballantine. 2004.

Dealing with failure. *Fast Company.* 9/2003.

Failure. *Fast Company.com.* 5/2001.

Great gigs. *Fast Company.* 6/2004.

Grow into success: http://www.topachievement.com/loustoops.html.

No buts. *How to Win Friends and Influence People,* by Dale Carnegie. Pocket. (Reissued edition). 1990.

Perspective please. *We got fired and it is the best thing that ever happened to us,* by Harvey MacKay. Ballantine. 2004.

Play to your strengths. *Fast Company,* 5/2001.

Reward failure. *Lessons from the Top: The search for America's Best Business Leaders,* by Thomas J. Neff and James M. Citrin. Doubleday. 1999.

Spectacular flops. P.J. O'Rourke. *The Success of Failure. The Atlantic Monthly.* 6/2002.

That's what business friends are for. *We Got Fired and It Is the Best Thing That Ever Happened to Us,* by Harvey MacKay. Ballantine. 2004.

Tough times build character. *Fast Company.* 5/2001.

What we do wrong. http://www.thejourneyfilm.com/journeyfilm/photo_30.htm.

22. The Future

Anticipating. *Fast Company.* 6–7/1998.

Accepting the future. *Fast Company.* 6/2000.

A company's worst enemy. *Fast Company.* 6/1999.

"A damn fine time to be alive." *Fast Company.* 5/2001.

"Dream it, you can do it." A sign hanging at Epcot Center in Florida.

Entrepreneurs everywhere. *Fast Company.* 6/2002.

The future calls. *Fast Company.* 3/2005.

The new world order. *Fast Company.* 9/2000.

Mosquito power. A column she wrote for Startups.co.uk http:// www.startups.co.uk/YVItzX5o1CPR9g.html. 12/2004.

Profit is like breathing. *Leading Is an Art*, by Max DePree. Dell. 1990.

Progress. *Fast Company.* 9/1999.

Reinvention. *Fast Company.* 6/2004.

The return of emotion. *Fast Company.* 10/1999.

Shaping the future. *Fast Company.* 12/1998.

Tomorrow. *Fast Company.* 6/2000.

Viva the revolution. *Rules for Revolutionaries: The Capitalist Manifesto for Creating and Marketing New Products and Services,* by Guy Kawasaki. HarperBusiness. 2000.

We have only just begun. *The Future of Work. How the New Order of Business Will Shape Your Organization, Your Management Style, and Your Life,* by Thomas W. Malone. Harvard Business School Press. 2004.

Why pessimists make lousy leaders. A speech entitled "Personal Renewal" delivered to McKinsey & Company, in Phoenix, AZ. November 10, 1990.

Index of Quote Titles

Index of Authors

12/05 (3713)